HOLIDAY HOMES

HOLIDAY HOMES

NONIE NIESEWAND

HENRY HOLT AND COMPANY
NEW YORK

Published in the United States by
Henry Holt and Company, Inc., 521 Fifth Avenue,
New York, New York 10175

Designed and produced by
Conran Octopus Limited
28-32 Shelton Street
London WC2 9PH

ISBN: 0-8050-0468-8

First American Edition

Printed in Hong Kong

10 9 8 7 6 5 4 3 2 1

ISBN 0-8050-0468-8

AUTHOR'S ACKNOWLEDGMENTS

To my sons, Oliver and James, the best companions on holiday, and at home. Before they were eight, they had trekked on foot across the Himalayas to the borders of Tibet which, they still insist, was not a holiday. To the team at Conran Octopus who all summer resisted the temptation to pack up this book and take a holiday. A collective thank you is due to the owners and their architects who invited us to step inside these holiday homes; to the publishing team in Australia who commissioned the picture stories: June McCallum, editor-in-chief of 'Australian Vogue' and 'Vogue Living' with Patricia Watson, Dorinda Hancock and Sandy Delves. Thank you to the translators Michela Albarello and Hilu Ginger for speedy and accurate work, and Liz Nichols who gave me unfailing support.

CONTENTS

HOLIDAY HOMES

Few things are as compulsive as time off. Escaping to an idyllic spot somewhere, sometime, is irresistible to most people, while the thought of escaping to your own home in that perfect setting is even more alluring. This book will lead you to the countryside, seaside, mountainside and waterside. The interiors explored are all stylish, yet with a down-to-earth approach to decoration that is typical of holiday homes. Not one is furnished in the formal grandeur of the inner city apartment, for they are homes shaped around the hobbies and enthusiasms of their part-time owners. Any home will benefit from the inspiring ideas and simple solutions they provide for carefree living. Those who are considering taking the plunge and buying a second home can enjoy a guided tour of every kind of holiday and weekend retreat and discover the advantages of the available options. There are practical points, too, which will help you to make the right choice and avoid problems. The armchair traveller can simply sit back and enjoy the beauty of some of the world's most exotic and exciting locations. Wish you were there?

CHAPTER ONE

COUNTRYSIDE

The countryside has a special poignancy. Our urge to escape to it is rooted firmly in the past, when our ancestors worked on the land and lived off the produce. Although we have lost many of these skills, and cemented over a great deal of the verdant countryside, the deep-seated longing for a rural retreat remains.

One beach may be like another, but the landscape differs from region to region. Picture prairie wheatlands where the tallest point on the skyline is a windmill, or lemon-scented terraces above a Mediterranean vineyard, or lush English meadows dotted with daisies and dairy herds. In each area the dwellings are as different as the view, for local materials and skills are used for building them. A simple country cottage may be made of flint and slate or local stone; it may be weatherboarded with pantiles or plastered and washed with the palest colour beneath a rush thatch.

Country properties, whether they are remote farmhouses or village cottages, are seldom called holiday homes since country communities and customs readily absorb newcomers — often regular weekend visitors who rapidly put down roots, and readily become settled in their surroundings, safe in the knowledge that property developers are unlikely to build anonymous holiday apartments nearby.

A country home doesn't need to be grandly decorated; comfort and simplicity are the essential elements. A house that is plainly furnished is less likely to be a target for burglars who break into houses left empty for long periods. In this chapter you will discover rooms in which comfortable furniture, soft furnishings in the potpourri colours of the countryside, and the odd treasure of sentimental value, have resolved their differences to give a sense of comfort and ease. Even the country manor, the eighteenth-century folly or the Californian post-modernist pavilion show the same measured informality and charm of the holiday home in tune with its surroundings. Colourful plants from the garden are set on a windowsill, bringing it into focus; baskets brim with ripe fruit from the orchard, jars of fresh honey are lined up on the kitchen table, hats and hampers are left in the hall, saddles and

Previous page: Barn in western Finland

harnesses by the stable – all indications of the work and pleasure taken in country activities.

If you want complete isolation, you will also take on the problems and additional·expense that a remote dwelling can entail. If it is far from the madding crowd, it is also likely to be some distance from the electricity or gas repair man, or newsagent. You may also have a lengthy drive to the pharmacy, or the shop for that essential ingredient for cooking. Easy access to village life will give you a sense of the community spirit, and local social events may provide alternatives to quiet evenings in front of the fire. The pleasures of feeling part of country life will provide the contrast you need to a hectic urban existence.

Anyone considering buying abroad will have a range of choices. If you are truly fascinated by a particular country, and have some knowledge of the language, a keen interest in its history and customs, and take pleasure in its cuisine and lifestyle, then you are ideally suited to a second home abroad. You will not feel out of place in a small village where the locals will warm to you because you can communicate in their language, as well as understand and respect their way of life. But even in a country familiar to you, there is the daunting prospect of searching for the ideal district, avoiding the pitfalls of falling for a place during an idyllic holiday only to find its charms wearing thin after a few visits.

City dwellers must beware of the lure of the countryside. It may seem totally absorbing and relaxing on the occasional weekend away with friends, or when staying in a well-appointed and historic country house hotel, but buying a house there is a different matter. A second home is a major financial commitment so you will want to use it for most of your hard-won annual vacations and weekends. Find a holiday home in the country if you are prepared to become involved in the community, and enjoy outdoor activites, whatever the weather. If you also appreciate an evening in front of the fire, or in the local pub or bar, away from lively night spots, then the countryside is the place for you.

Statistics on the resale of property show that the most successful holiday homes are those that are inland, near a village and have been chosen because the owners admire the style of building. People tire more quickly of modern condominiums and houses bought because of their proximity to a leisure centre or sporting facility.

If you like country pursuits and village life, you may be tempted by a derelict building of great character and potential, such as a barn or farmhouse, at an attractive purchase price. Bargains do exist, but finding one involves concentrated research. Restoring a derelict building may cost as much again as the purchase price.

To find the perfect country retreat, take your time. Choose the area you want to be in, and visit it as often as possible before you make your final decision about the precise district. Get to know the people who live

Gîte in Normandy, France

there permanently as well as any other holiday home-owners.

Local inhabitants are going to be a source of essential information. They may even help you find suitable properties. When you have moved in they can recommend reliable builders and restorers, secondhand furniture retailers, caretakers and guardians, cleaners and gardeners. Get to know your local bartender, publican or small shop keeper and you will have a useful friend. Since these places are open long hours, and know the district and its people, they can help in many ways and perhaps become the keyholders for those who rent your house, or do repairs on it.

Consider the location of the property: are there any factories, workshops or playing fields nearby that could disturb your peaceful seclusion? If the house is near farmland, find out who owns it and when crops are sprayed. Find out about any development in the area, such as roads, factories or more houses.

If you fall for a remote, traditional property, make sure it has essential services – the cost of installing running water, drainage, electricity and telephone wires to an isolated building may dull your enthusiasm. Consider access as well: a rough track may be just bumpy in fine weather, but impassable after a storm.

Being isolated not only means getting away from the crowds, but also from shops, hospitals, police and services. Bear in mind extra costs when calling in builders and repairmen, too.

Renovation will be slow, since you are dependent on local builders who seldom consider a part-time home-owner a priority on their schedule. In Europe, the local town hall will help you to find artisans who are experts in sympathetic restoration of period buildings, both inside and out. Use personal recommendations, get references and obtain itemized estimates from more than one builder or artisan. Pay in stages once work is underway.

RENTING OUT

Renting out your holiday home may seem to be a sure way of financing it. This is not always the case.
- If your holiday home is abroad, there may be restrictions on letting it. Find out about this before you purchase the property.
- Work out the estimated level of return, taking into account the going rate for renting similar properties, any tax payable on the income, special insurance requirements and other extra costs.
- You can expect your property to deteriorate more quickly if rented out and therefore to require more maintenance, so build this into your calculations.
- For the highest financial return, it is best to rent your property privately, advertising in a major national or international newspaper.
- Arrangements must be made for the property to be cleaned, and for someone to act as a caretaker, who will hold the keys, as well as deal with any problems or emergencies.
- Give as much information as you can to tenants, including detailed maps of the area and advice on shopping and services. Leave a house book in the property explaining every detail from operating the water heater to unblocking the drains and locking up. Remember that if the tenants disturb your neighbours or behave badly, it will reflect on you and could affect your relationship with the locals. Avoid this by laying down rules on such things as loud music, parties, and parking.
- An organization or agent who will let the property for you will take commission, but will save you time and inconvenience. Contact the Federation of Overseas Property and Development, or another reputable international organization before selecting a company. Often companies can arrange cleaners, a laundry service and even a cook, as well as offer your tenants assistance with travel.

1

ENGLISH COUNTRY HOUSE

One of the myths of the English country house is that it was a comfortable place to stay. In the eighteenth and nineteenth centuries letters home from guests were full of complaints about the cold and the need to retire early to bed with a warming pan filled with coals. So it is pleasing to see how many of these recalcitrant old houses have been coaxed into the twentieth century with modern appliances and comforts, such as central heating, without losing any of their original charm and style.

The English reluctance to call a country house a holiday home, even when it is used only for weekends and holidays, may be ascribed to the regularity with which the family return to their country house, as well as to their easy familiarity with country customs.

This charming Leicestershire farmhouse,

1 *House and front garden*
2 *Herb garden*

3

with its cottage-style garden, reflects both ease and enjoyment. Despite the casual appearance, both house and garden were drawn up to a masterplan, designed for carefree holiday living, by professional decorator John Stefanidis and garden designer Arabella Lennox-Boyd. In the midsummer sun, with the horses grazing in the fields beyond, the garden is a profusion of colour, contained within old-fashioned brick walls and borders.

The mellowed brick which gives the house its welcoming warmth, is echoed in the garden paths, and in the farmhouse kitchen. As in the old English nursery rhyme about the three little pigs who built a house to keep out an intruder – in their case, a wolf – the brick house is a solid structure that will withstand a great deal of huffing and puffing in inclement weather.

Arabella Lennox-Boyd used a radial plan for the garden, so that the house is encircled in a web of pattern and colour. She designed the circular herb garden in a wheel shape, set like brick sun-rays. Overlooked from the kitchen window, it contains a variety of herbs for culinary use. The wall around it was built with old bricks, scavenged from a local demolition site, which is often a good place to pick up raw materials.

Architect Nicholas Johnston linked the original farmhouse to a barn to provide well-proportioned space for a large open-plan kitchen, with quarry-tiled floor and unplastered, whitewashed walls. The line of labour-saving appliances is fitted inconspicuously: arched feeding troughs, originally used for cattle, form the base of the large sink and work surfaces. The fridge and other cumbersome white fittings are camouflaged behind wooden door fronts.

In the country house kitchen, functional appliances are not always sympathetic, but space-age streamlining can be avoided. A dresser full of china plates, open shelving for cookery books and utensils, copper pots hung on the wall, and a double sink in the butler style give the room a timeless character.

John Stefanidis' decoration pulls together the gentle colours of the English country house and anchors them in the drawing room with a buttercup yellow sofa and hand-blocked Indian cushions. His interiors have a personal quality that interprets the enthusiasms of the owners and highlights his own impeccable sense of proportion and space. Here, too, contemporary features like the radiators are hidden. Little of the twentieth century intrudes in this peaceful setting, which is nonetheless geared to modern living.

3   *Sitting room*
4   *Kitchen*

1

2

CALIFORNIAN PAVILIONS

The Californian home of post-modernist architect Charles Jencks is a playful celebration of the four elements – earth, air, fire and water (*terra, aer, ignis* and *aqua* in the classical order). They inspire a theme of symbolism that is enshrined in the main ranch house and all seven of the pavilions, set in a wooded garden. He has landscaped the *terra*, filled the outdoor pool and jacuzzi with *aqua*, and chosen to interpret *aer* and *ignis* as the view and the sun, worshipped by Californians and hedonists the world over.

The inspiration for this architectural exercise was the mythical poetry of John Milton, whose opening stanzas are inscribed upon the timber frames and rafters in an attempt to bring rusticity to inner city life. Bored by the austerity of modernist architecture, which makes use of industrial components, Jencks has reinterpreted classical forms in his own way, using rough-hewn wood as his basic material. Nature is suggested in every trellis, terrace or pergola of this unconventional summerhouse. The pavilions, set amongst acacia and eucalyptus trees, have slender tree-like columns painted brown, lavender and turquoise.

The guest pavilion is the seventh building (seven being a sacred and mystical number in mythology), called the Hermitage, which was celebrated by Milton as the scholar's retreat. Jencks describes it as a 'primitive hut', similar to a monastic cell, and guests who have slept here value its contemplative calm. Planned upon the simple geometric order of the cross, it is illuminated by the daylight that floods in through the skylight and the clerestory windows. At night, the room is lit by the fan-shaped lights on either side of the bed. The Gothic-style bed, designed by Jencks, reinforces the

1 *The Hermitage, or guest pavilion*
2 *Hermitage bedroom*

3

cloistered image, as does the high ceiling that is detailed with a trellised dado rail.

In Jencks' architectural scheme, the garden also reflects an appreciation of Milton's poetry. The red, pink and white plantings are a celebration of the joyous world of *L'Allegro*, while the shady glades recall *Il Penseroso*. Trellis gates lead to the swimming pool. Its jagged brick edge outlines the shape of the state of California, and symbolizes the rupture line, since the pool lies upon a tributary of the San Andreas fault. A smaller pavilion, like a timber portico, holds the hot tub, above which is stencilled the appropriate heading 'Aquaquaquaqu'. This

message, part classical and part Disneyland, suggests to Jencks a quacking duck.

The timber frame car port, with black steel supports and storage tanks of grey and green, is another lighthearted attempt to bring Milton's rustic symbolism to the city of Los Angeles, where the car is worshipped. On the timber joists of the temple-shaped garage are the opening lines of Milton's *L'Allegro*. The 'horrid shapes and shrieks and sights unholy' is a cryptic reference to the cars and metal rubbish bins that are housed here.

3 *Swimming pool and hot tub pavilion*
4 *Car port*

4

1

2

MARIGOLD COTTAGE, SUSSEX

Guests who alight at Marigold Cottage, set in its own pretty garden, seldom detect anything unusual in its external appearance. However, once inside the long interior, its origins are hard to disguise. Marigold Cottage is the final destination for two railway carriages.

Since 1921 they have been used as a holiday home and Tim Stephens, the present owner, has researched their history. The carriages were both built in 1901, one as a picnic saloon, the other as an inspection carriage to accompany the royal entourage. They last ran along the tracks in France during the First World War, when one became a hospital carriage, the other apparently part of the original headquarters train for Earl Haig. The picnic saloon is now used as a bedroom and bathroom; the inspection saloon is a dining room.

Life aboard a train needs careful planning and organization and there were several things the Stephens had to consider when furnishing the place. In the original train, seating was invariably arranged down the sides of the coach, with a series of flap-top tables fixed to the central aisle. Nowadays most pieces of furniture are placed centre stage to take into account the arched roof with its bow-hoop canopy. In the bedroom, the double bed is set in the middle of the room so that the wall behind frames it. A sunny conservatory, that is used as a living room, lets light into the other rooms through the carriage entrances. The doors and windows, added in 1972, were gleaned from a Victorian railway station.

The railway carriages have come to rest at Middleton, tucked behind tamarisk trees and the medieval sea wall. These charming relics of the Edwardian age, imaginatively converted to an unusual and informal holiday home, sit comfortably in the English countryside, a short distance from the village.

1 *Cottage and garden*
2 *Living room*
3 *Bedroom*

3

1

2

FARMHOUSE IN SPAIN

Any serious restoration work of old buildings involves making use of period features, whether they are feeding troughs for animals, bread ovens set in the stone chimney breast or a hand-drawn water pump. Restoring these intrinsic features to the building, while finding a practical role for them in the house, is a challenge.

This house at the end of the village of Madremanya, in the Catalan region of Spain, is a showpiece of simple but imaginative adaptation. The farmhouse had been standing empty for 20 years when Hugo Curletto and Arnaud Maty Lavauzelle rescued it. A pig pen in the basement (an unlikely structure for inclusion in a modern holiday home) was converted into a shower cubicle, and an old meat safe, with its lower doors removed, was turned into a display cabinet. Outside, on the flagstone terrace, trees provide dappled shade without blocking the view of the rolling hills.

The centre of all Catalan farms is the vast arched hall that leads to the ground floor rooms. Farm carts and agricultural tools were once stored here. The new owners, sensitive to the origins of the house, decided not to alter this monastic space, with its rough plastered walls covered in a pale wash. The basic furniture – wooden boxes and bench – were discovered in the central hall, and were polished up and left in repose. These provide the warm hues in a cool interior. All that was added to this peaceful courtyard was a pair of lamps and some Moroccan mats on the floor.

It was essential to keep the arches since they balance the inner space and emphasize the fine proportions of the room. At the far side of the hall the openings lead to a hidden wine cellar which has still to be converted, although a use for it has not yet been decided.

Returning the house to its

1 *Central hall*
2 *Blue bedroom*

3

natural colours was another of the main tasks. Regional colours are often determined by the landscape and it is common in some parts of the world for handfuls of earth to be scooped up and stirred into a lime wash to colour it. In Catalonia, the reddish earth gives a pinkish tinge to surfaces, such as the ceiling in the kitchen of the farmhouse.

Traditionally, the blue of the Mediterranean is supposed to repel insects, so many interior surfaces are washed with this colour. Two blues of varying intensity are used in a bedroom: a soft blue for the walls and a deep blue for the skirting boards, which is picked up in the woven Spanish bedspread and the lamp base. This colour scheme is both calming and cooling when the sun is at its fiercest.

Much of the nineteenth-century furniture was already in the house when the new owners moved in. The ornately carved bedhead, with scrollwork defined in charcoal lines, was discovered in one of the six bedrooms. A muslin net, as effective against winged insects as the traditional blue paint, is loosely and simply draped over the bed.

The kitchen is an old settled place with terracotta flagged floors, and rose washed walls. The mellow brick shelves display green and white china from Bisbal. Nothing in this kitchen is merely decorative; even the traditional Catalan fireplace and bread oven are used today. The old-fashioned bread bins, and the rustic chairs with rush seats were found locally. Country fairs and markets can be a treasure trove for second-hand furniture and local craftwork. Such items are often inexpensive and highly suitable for furnishing a holiday home abroad.

The new owners, holidaying in a closed rural community, made an effort to introduce themselves to the ways of the country, absorbing local custom and observing tradition in the restoration of their second home.

3 *Terrace*
4 *Kitchen*

4

1

2

3

GYPSY CARAVAN

If you are out walking in the English or Irish countryside on a fine day, you may come across an encampment of painted wagons in a copse, a skewbald horse tethered nearby. Today, the caravans are more likely to house holiday-makers than gypsies, although Chris Hill, the owner of this one, does sell a few back to the Romany folk.

The urge to shed cares and possessions and take off on the road appeals to the gypsy in all of us, but tagging a heavyweight caravan onto the back of the car and setting off for a convenient site is not everyone's idea of a carefree holiday. The horse-drawn gypsy caravan offers a more romantic escapade. Chris Hill has vivid memories of travelling bands of gypsies in the home counties of his boyhood. Always fascinated by them, he gave up his city job to restore and sell authentic wagons.

The first gypsy homes were bender tents, which were loaded onto the back of a donkey or cart. Hazel rods were arched over and covered with felt, which was then pinned together with blackthorn spikes. This shape possibly provided inspiration for the bowed canopy of the first wagons – a design still followed today. The bows are bent over from one side of the vehicle to the other, then covered with a thick carpet for insulation, and a canvas sheet for protection. The front and back are boarded up with a rib and matchboard construction.

Palatial interiors, like this one, became important to the Romany community, who favoured gilding. Deep burgundy, claret or forest green were favourite colours for the exterior paintwork. Even the shafts that harness the horse are elaborately carved and painted.

In these flamboyant caravans every surface is adorned, with cut glass, etched glass panels and chamfered woodwork. Symbols carved in the wood, and etched or painted on the panels usually feature clusters of fruit, and the horse much loved by gypsy travellers. Rose-coloured fabric, pencil pleated and hung round the edges of the interior, brings a luxurious cosy glow, as well as insulation, to the inside of the caravan.

Chris Hill has never found a wagon furnished in a decorative style more recent than the Art Nouveau of the 1900s. The interior design is usually inspired by Victoriana and early twentieth-century arts and crafts. He has remained true to the originals, seeking out specialist craftsmen capable of restoring these mobile homes to their past splendour.

1 *Exterior of caravan*
2 *Kitchen area*
3 *Berth*

FRENCH FARMSTEAD

The Dutch family who restored these rambling farm buildings on a hilltop in north Périgord, made good use of local knowledge and experience – a lesson for anyone buying a holiday home abroad. They employed builders and craftsmen from the region to carry out the work because they felt that they would restore the house sympathetically, and in the traditional way.

Périgord is in the southern part of the Dordogne region. The area is noted for its fertile farmland, truffles, walnut trees, and the remote farmhouses scattered throughout the countryside. This 100-year-old farmhouse was derelict when found. It was jointly owned by members of a family who had been feuding for 20 years. Rooms once used to pen in animals at night were dank and tiny, and so dark that you could barely see inside them. When the roof had been repaired with old tiles, found locally, the house was opened up and space allocated for the various rooms. The plastered walls were sponged with a honey colour which reflects the mellow tones of such a region, where tobacco is left to dry in barns, pumpkins ripen on window sills and, when the leaves start to fall, the truffle rooting season begins.

The farmhouse kitchen/diner, built by a local carpenter, has a staircase down to the basement, which has been converted to a shower room. This makes use of the same plumbing system as the kitchen. A living room was built downstairs, and the master bedroom upstairs; guest bedrooms are housed in one of the barns. Another staircase climbs up to the attic, where there are a number of spare beds for extra visitors.

Two of the main priorities of a holiday home are light and ventilation. The owners resisted the temptation to replace all the old windows with new ones, as this would have ruined the appearance of the house and in no way added to its charm. Only one

1 *Farm buildings and terrace*

1

2

new window was added in the living room, because the interior was so dark, but it was carefully chosen to resemble the rest.

As entrances can also affect the appearance of a house, rotten doors were replaced with new ones. These are left ajar in summer to let the sunlight stream into the rooms. The inside of the house was very carefully restored: new beams were chosen to match the old ones, and chestnut floorboards were laid underfoot. Furniture was picked up at local junk shops, called *brocantes*. The fitted wooden shutters, stained a reddish walnut colour, are practical and will deter intruders when the house is empty.

A terrace, modelled on local examples, was added to the front of the house. Built by the owners with cement, and stones from the Dordogne marked in a mosaic pattern, it provides a place for sitting in the sun or dining out. A terracotta tiled floor marks the transition from the terrace to the inside of the house.

An effect of secluded cosiness is achieved in one of the bedrooms with careful

decoration. Because of the small windows the room could be cold and dimly lit, but instead the pretty patterned wallpaper and warm colours of the furnishings give it a rosy glow. The windows are given prominence with a drape casually tied in a loose knot. This allows daylight to filter through, while a large mirror reflects the light in the room and creates a feeling of more space. The bright patchwork quilt and cushions on the painted brass bedstead bring pattern and colour into a room that appears to dance with light.

In every room, small touches add to the relaxed atmosphere of the house and give some indication of the owners' interests. Bunches of fresh flowers from the garden and surrounding countryside are placed in jugs, straw hats and baskets adorn the backs of chairs and cupboards, jars of honey cover the kitchen table and a telescope is kept to hand for observing the clear night sky.

2 *Corner of living room*
3 *Kitchen*
4 *Bedroom*

TRIUMPHAL ARCH IN NORFOLK

English architect, Nicholas Hills, who lives with his family over a triumphal arch in Norfolk, makes the point that a holiday home often insidiously works its way into your life to become your principal place of residence. Most people buy holiday homes with retirement in mind, but Nicholas Hills found that his work, renovating grand English country houses, drew him to live in his unusual holiday home.

The triumphal arch was built in the eighteenth century as a frontispiece to a grand Palladian house. It was erected by Thomas Coke, later first Earl of Leicester, as part of the 'approach and distant decoration' to his family seat. The arch had been built on land held only on lease and it was the first Countess, Margaret Tufton, who later bought three acres from Christ's College, Cambridge, in order to 'secure the said

1 *Southern approach*
2 *Main room, or saloon*

2

arch' and the house, and keep them in good order when the Earl of Leicester died.

At treetop level, amidst the rustling ilex, the building has spectacular views of the countryside. Walls, more than two feet thick, form the great rusticated arch. The giant overhanging stone cornice suggests a monumental fragment of ancient Rome.

The first drawings of the elevation were made by William Kent in 1734, showing only a slit window beneath a large inscription panel. However, the stone mason, Matthew Brettingham, omitted part of Kent's design in favour of a symmetrical plan, and enlarged the windows to a semi-circular shape. Building bricks were made from local clay and fired on the estate; flint from nearby fields was used for the panels of the arch.

In the 1970s when Nicholas Hills discovered the triumphal arch, boarded up and derelict, only the roof was sound. The ceilings had gone, leaving the roof structure exposed. This effect, which Nicholas Hills rather liked, forms a pediment inside the room, as well as outside, and produces a

harmonious and agreeable space. He used part of it for a mezzanine floor, like a gallery, and put in a shower and dressing room at this new level. Repair work involved the installation of plaster boards and insulation materials between the rafters in the arch room. This saloon (as Nicholas Hills refers to it), high above the drive, has windows facing in four directions and serves as a general living and entertaining room. Oyster shells, mutton bones, and broken claret bottles, which were discovered when floorboards were lifted to lay water pipes, give some indication of past jollities.

The Hills have composed an unlikely but perfectly manageable home. The saloon is connected to one wing, forming a unit with the ground floor kitchen that is used today as much as it was then. Apart from replacing an earth closet at the foot of the stairs with an up-to-date version, the building functions in much the same way as it did over two centuries ago. There is no electric light, but oil lamps, storm lanterns and candles light the interiors. A

local blacksmith crafted the twelve-branch candelabra, and made a copy of the original storm lanterns used at the house. In the saloon, the only heat is from a log fire in the corner fireplace, with extra warmth radiating from the Aladdin oil lamps.

Daylight streams through the narrow windows that seem to suit the scale of the interiors so well. The kitchen has four of these windows, and each bedroom has two. The saloon windows are framed by generous swathes of natural cotton hung from poles, and tied back with khaki silk ropes. Brick walls, formerly plastered but now painted a cream colour, have a plain rusticity which contrasts admirably with some of the grand decoration.

In the main arch room, the curve of the semi-circular windows on each façade is echoed in the circular sofa. This is four quarters of foam, topped with a feather squab, which fold together to form a semi-circular seat, or open out to make a bed. This main room was once used as sleeping quarters for two families who lived in the arch.

Furnishing the room was

not as effortless as it appears. All the furniture had to be manoeuvred up the stone spiral staircase which winds up from one corner of the structure, a green velvet-clad handrail following its ascent. The unusual obelisk bookcases were also made in four sections. Books can be fitted in from both sides and, as the obelisk is wider at the bottom and narrower at the top, it is suitable for a variety of book sizes.

Furnishings in the top room, picked up at country house sales, are in sympathy with the classical building. There are plaster busts of Homer and the Belvedere Apollo, possibly taken from casts that were collected by Brettingham's son when he travelled to Italy for Lord Leicester. The stags' antlers on either side, which add to the hunting lodge style, also came from a sale. A print collection of famous triumphal arches includes two representations of triumphs from the Arch of Titus in Rome.

3 Dining room from the doorway

3

1

DESERT DWELLING

The awesome rocks of the Arizona desert dictated the design of this extraordinary house. The owners, who lived in Washington D.C., over 1400 miles away, were fascinated by the history of the region. They bought a plot of land and were lucky enough to find an architect – Charles Forman Johnson – who was sympathetic to their idea of building a house here. As soon as he saw the land he realized that the house would have to be imbedded in the rocks, rather than built alongside them. He took photographs from every angle and asked a friend to pose beside the rocks so that he could assess the scale. Later on, aerial photographs were taken of the site for reference.

Charles Johnson lived and worked in Santa Fe and had designed many houses there in the Spanish colonial style. He based his design for the desert house on the traditional hacienda buildings of New Mexico, but instead of using clay for the walls, he specified concrete, mounted on the stone. A huge block of granite forms the west wall of the house, and the surrounding rocks are sculpted into cavernous rooms and courtyards on twelve different levels. Natural fissures in the rock face are fitted with glass to provide irregular slit windows.

In this oddly shaped and sculpted house, no wall is straight, no ceiling horizontal. Huge pine beams, called *vigas*, are used to support the pine ceiling, and walls with rounded edges and hand-rendered surfaces reflect a Hispanic heritage.

Furniture for the house was chosen with restraint. The floors were rendered smooth in contrast to the uneven walls, and natural materials were used throughout. Having once lived in a city 'shoe box', the owners love the warmth and smoothness of their rock house and the way the light plays on it, casting shadows inside.

1 *House in the desert*
2 *Living room*

SWEDISH SUMMERHOUSE

This wooden farmhouse, outside Stockholm, dates back to the early seventeenth century. Since medieval times Scandinavian houses have been built with a timber frame, brick and mortar clad walls and a clay tiled roof. A modern version, which packs flat for speedy on-site assembly, is popular for contemporary holiday homes throughout the world.

For 200 years this house belonged to the Swedish Royal Navy, but today only its name, 'Seaman's House', and the ship's barometer behind the cooking range, record its past. It is one of the few original houses still standing above a narrow bay, in the midst of fields that yield strawberries, mushrooms and wild flowers.

Seaman's House has only three rooms. A small entrance leads into a living room (used for working and dining), a kitchen and a tiny bedroom that is more like a sailor's bunk. Lars and Gunnel Bünge-Meyer, who holiday here every summer, have chosen a decorative scheme that is reminiscent of nineteenth-century Swedish provincial interiors.

The furniture, such as the wooden sideboard with drawers and cupboards, and the plain pine and beech tables and chairs, is modest and functional. With its wide plank pine floors, planed and scrubbed, pale pink and blue papered walls and match-boarded ceiling above the white painted rafters, this little cottage gives the impression of being more spacious than it is.

The fresh charm and simplicity is a theme carried through the house. There are blue and white gingham curtains at the windows, and striped woven rugs on the bare floorboards. Wallpaper, with a small sprig motif, covers up rough plaster or cracks and introduces a delicate pattern to the otherwise plain interior. In the land of the midnight sun, light floods into this holiday home all summer long.

1 *House and meadow*
2 *Dining area*
3 *Kitchen*

CHAPTER TWO

SEASIDE

The sea has a natural pull that draws you to it. Simply hold a seashell to your ear and you can almost hear the whisper of the ocean. Your holiday memories may be of the limpid waters of the Mediterranean, the archipelagos of the Baltic, exploring the rock pools of the Atlantic, or roaming the sandy beaches of the Caribbean or the Pacific. Whatever the coastline, the urge to return to familiar shores is strong in all of us.

Anyone who lives by the sea wants to overlook it, so seaside houses tend to make a feature of large windows and sliding doors that lead to the terrace, patio or sundeck, opening up the view and providing shelter when drawn across on blustery days. Holidaymakers at the seaside spend a great deal of time in the fresh air, and homes are designed around an outdoor life: a table set beneath the vine, a pavilion under the trees, a barbecue on the terrace for grilling the day's catch, an umbrella and chairs on the sundeck. The clear light and splendid sunrises and sunsets that occur at the seaside often inspire a vivid use of colour, both inside and out. In the stark light of northern Denmark, houses on the peninsula of Skagen are painted in warm colours; on the African coast, the earth tones of ochre and siena offset the stark white of the Moroccan villas, while in the south of France, bold blues and yellow echo the sand, sea and sky.

Seaside towns are many and varied. Quaint fishing villages have the atmosphere of a small country community enhanced by the romance and adventure of the sea and the people who live beside it. Finding an old house with a sea view is not easy: if your dream is to renovate a derelict historic building with character, you will need to invest a lot in it, since it may have been uninhabited for some time or have been battered by the elements. Seek out a fishing village with old lanes and a harbour which has not yet been discovered and developed and you may find a bargain there.

There is room for innovation, if not renovation, at the seaside, with some of the most beautiful sites in the world offered to architects who can design buildings to make the most of light and space. A house built to your own specifications could be the answer to securing a place close to a seaside

Previous page: Mustique

fishing village. Find a site which is available for development and check the percentage of the land that can be built on, and whether or not adjoining land is also to be developed. Your chosen architect will be able to estimate the schedule, cost of labour materials, and deal with planning permission, access and essential services. However, no one should underestimate the amount of work. Consider the upheaval caused by building work on an established home, and multiply it several times. You may be one of the increasing number of intrepid home builders who spend their weekends toiling on their own site while living in a small town apartment. Dedication and exhausting physical exertion could appeal to you if the end product is the house of your dreams, but talk at length to an architect and a builder and face the reality of this awesome task before even considering it.

Holiday apartments cater for those looking for a place in the sun in a modern resort that has purpose-built developments. Close to marinas, or perhaps a famous golf course, these estates offer modern architecture, good security and maintenance, with on-the-spot recreational facilities. Seaside resorts, built in the nineenth century for the wealthy, have promenades and bandstands, botanical gardens and elegant buildings. Many of these – in the south of France or parts of northern Europe – still offer sophisticated leisure facilities as well as converted, up-to-date apartments behind gracious façades.

Whatever the location – shingled or sandy beach, tidal estuary, clifftop or lagoon – holiday homes by the sea are always susceptible to the changes in weather. Whether they are clad in weatherboard (a popular style in the United States and Australia), in brick or stone, or cement with a protective paint finish, they present a tough exterior, as watertight as an oilskin. For the wind that fills the yachtsman's sails will also shower seafront houses with salt spray and blast them with sand in a storm; the sun that tans the skin will have a yellowing effect on a house that is too exposed to the elements. Inside, surface finishes need to be heavy duty, furniture light and functional, and furnishing materials, such as cotton, canvas and jute, made to last.

Traditional seaside dwellings built for fishermen, coastguards and lighthouse keepers, may have a superb location and sea views, but they can be expensive to convert for modern living. (See Countryside, page 10, for further information on traditional holiday homes.)

The large developments of purpose-built villas and apartments that line the coast in many holiday resorts are often ideal for a time-share venture (see also Mountainside, page 88). You get what you pay for in terms of building quality, attractive site, outdoor areas, privacy and security. Luxury beach condominiums offer superb sports facilities, many of them specializing in one sport such as golf or tennis, with professional coaching. Some have their own yachting marinas, swimming pools and shops. Many also provide clubs and bars for a lively nightlife. Avoid the villa next to the discotheque.

House in Skagen, Denmark

A modern villa on a good development may lack character but it is a sound investment because it will be easy to resell and maintain. Your property is managed in your absence; sites are secure and safe; facilities are provided for children of all ages. All this is reflected in the purchase and maintenance price.

Avoid buying an unfinished building or part of an unfinished site. There is no guarantee it will ever be completed. When visiting a development, never be tempted to part with money until you have fully investigated the property and the land you are buying, and have sought legal advice. Do not fall for the ploy that unless you put down a deposit immediately you will lose your chance to purchase a villa.

Many resorts are lively for a short season each year and then turn into ghost towns. Visit a place at different times of the year before committing yourself. This is true of any holiday home and is an important reason why you should not buy a property while on holiday. A clifftop cottage or seafront apartment may be freezing cold in winter, or overlook the mudflats of a tidal estuary at neap tide. Even if you want to use your property only in the high season, you may want to let it at other times.

Seaside houses take a battering from the elements. The sun and salt that ages your skin can have a similar effect on paintwork, causing peeling and yellowing. Sealants and weather-resistant undercoats will help protect bricks, mortar and woodwork. Exterior surfaces can be jet sprayed with heavy duty paint over an acrylic base to prevent peeling or flaking.

At the seaside, pests such as sand fleas may move in when the house is empty. Lay powder around skirting boards, or spray the area with pesticide, when you leave. An old-fashioned, but effective, deterrent is bunches of woodruff, strewn on the floor. Flyscreens and mosquito nets may be necessary in hot climates.

BUYING ABROAD

- Never buy a property without seeing it, or on the spur of the moment while on a holiday. Never part with money without legal advice.
- Buy through a recognized estate agent, preferably one based in your own country who specializes in property abroad.
- As soon as you have decided that you want to buy a particular property, get two lawyers involved in the transaction immediately. In your country of residence, find a law firm which specializes in buying property abroad. You will also need legal assistance in the country where you are buying the property. Ensure every legal document is translated and checked.
- Take legal advice on whether or not to get a survey. In your country of residence there will be an association of property surveyors who can put you in touch with reputable companies abroad.
- Get to know the locals because they will be your main source of information.
- Avoid buying an unfinished building or one that is part of an unfinished development.
- There may be restrictions on taking money out of the country where you are buying, and on foreigners buying property. Check immediately that you will be able to recoup your investment.
- Obtaining finance for your holiday home will be expensive, so take this into account. Consider all possibilities. Developers sometimes offer their own finance arrangements, although interest payments are often high.
- Take into account the cost of renovation, furnishing, legal fees, transfer costs and taxes. On a derelict building renovation work could double the initial purchase price.
- Extra costs include cleaning and care of the property when you are not there, making the place secure (see page 109) and, most importantly the cost of travelling to and from your holiday home and the time it takes.

HIDEAWAY IN THE WINDWARD ISLES

The remote Caribbean island of Mustique is a paradise of white sands and clear blue sea. No more than three miles long, it is privately owned and therefore protected from property speculators and tourist complexes. Twenty years ago Lord Glenconner asked the celebrated stage designer, Oliver Messel, to plan the architectural style for the island residences. This was a felicitous choice for such a dramatic setting, as a variety of styles could have ruined the appearance of the island. Messel chose to blend the traditional architecture of the plantation owners' houses with a theatrical attention to detail. It has given the buildings, against their exotic backdrop, an established, yet unconventional character.

This holiday home, sited on the lee of a hill amidst the ancient palms of the rain forest, is a fine example of Messel's craft. His ability to give a new house an antique patina means that few visitors to the island would guess that this one was built just 16 years ago. He specified simple building materials and used them to grand effect, both inside and out. The house is made of local coral stone, and the cement tiled roof stained to match. In the living room, cement was used again for the large floor tiles. A Regency-style chandelier hangs from the ceiling, which slopes inward from the corners making the intimate rooms appear spacious. For dramatic effect Messel blended rough and smooth, rustic and sophisticated, old and new to create a house of great charm Although the entrance to the house is splendidly proportioned, with pillars and porticos, the recessed archway entrance on the south side gives little indication of what lies beyond, in the best tradition of the theatre.

1 *House in the hills*
2 *Living room and dining area*
3 *View from the veranda*
4 *Veranda*

3

4

1

MOROCCAN SEASIDE VILLA

The Moorish villa is the longest surviving architectural style still found far from its native African shores. It is so widely copied that it is now hard to discover in its pure form. Few seaside homes today are built to a centuries-old plan, but the house at Cabo Negro is a gem; an authentic Moroccan villa which was built as a fortress on the shores of the Mediterranean, and is now a holiday home. Thick outer walls, shaped and smoothed in clay, then washed to a brilliant white, follow the lie of the land as naturally as a sea wall. Today, the traditional slit windows protect the occupants from the midday sun, rather than from an anticipated siege. The commanding exterior of the building is softened by the magenta bougainvillaea that spills over its walls and the lawns, planted with laurel bushes, that sweep down to the seashore.

Many forms of Arab architecture and design are influenced by the natural surroundings. Here, the ochre earth, the green pines and cacti and the brilliant blue sky suggest the colour schemes inside the house. Hexagonal terracotta tiles are covered with Islamic carpets of woven silk, kelims with interlaced coloured threads, and vegetable-dyed rugs in the earthy browns and sky blues of the African coastline.

No other building form hides as much from the outside, nor reveals so much once you are admitted. Each room opens out through lofty archways to secluded inner gardens, laid out in the Andalusian manner. There are courtyards with fountains, terraces for sunbathing, screened from passers-by, and a giant papyrus that clambers up to the balconies and arches. The owner, an enthusiastic gardener, has created an oasis of colour with geraniums, roses, morning glory, and sweet-scented jasmine.

An ancient studded door marks the entrance to the

1 *Walled terraces*
2 *Inner gardens and swimming pool*

2

3

house, where lanterns with multi-coloured glass panes guide the visitor into the cool interior. Built to an open plan, the different areas for seating, eating and sleeping are divided by partition walls and arches.

Near a patio planted with pale white flowers is a small inner sanctum furnished in shades of ivory and mother-of-pearl, illuminated at dusk by wrought iron lanterns. It is here that guests adjourn to sip mint tea during the intense heat of the afternoon. At night, the candles are lit in an adjoining room, furnished with deep red Tetouan fabrics, and coffee is served with local pastries called 'gazelle's horns'.

The large sitting room has traditional platform seating, scattered with silk cushions; a few collector's pieces of Syrian furniture, inlaid with mother-of-pearl, and handbeaten copper tables from the local *souk*, or market.

The arrangement of glass panes in the windows has become an architectural feature. Some of the panes have been placed horizontally rather than vertically to alter the pattern of light, but all of

them are lined up symmetrically in the well-proportioned rooms. Each square window has 17 panes of glass assembled on a grid as formal as a frieze, while arched windows are given fanlights. The purpose is two-fold: they are decorative yet burglar proof, with no single pane large enough for an intruder to slip through. Upon the recessed window ledges are hand-painted blue and green earthenware pots and plates from the Moroccan cities of Fez and Rabat.

This is a place of great contrast: open yet secluded, pale yet bright, warm yet cool. The thick walls of the house muffle any noise and keep the interiors cool in the midday heat. As dusk falls, these clay walls are still warm from the sun. The refreshing night air is heavy with the aroma of sweet jasmine and honeysuckle, the senses lulled by a richness of scent and texture.

3 *Arched doorway to
  sitting room*
4 *Windows and
  earthenware*
5 *Seating area*

1

BUNGALOWS ON THE BALTIC

On the wildest, most northerly tip of Denmark lies the salty seaside town of Skagen. Sited in a nature reserve, shaped rather like a bird's head, it is both heath and moorland with windswept sand dunes facing two seas – Skagerrak to the west and Kattegat to the east. Scenes of the sea and dunes, as well as portraits and interiors, were painted by turn-of-the-century Scandinavian artists who came to paint in this remarkable light. Their paintings show elegant holidaymakers alongside robust fisherfolk, and the bustling local hostelry,

Brondums (where Hans Christian Andersen once stayed), is still open to summer visitors today. Some of the other hotels that grew up for the artist community and their followers are now used as holiday apartments.

For over a century Skagen has been a busy harbour town with a fleet of trawlers, as well as a popular resort for Danes, many of whom own holiday homes here. Fishermen and holidaymakers alike have painted their shoreside homes in strong earthy colours of ochre, rust and leaf green, to refract the cold northern light.

The architecture of Skagen celebrates the sea, and the fishermen whose livelihood depends upon it. The

traditional fishermen's cottages have distinctive sheered gables and terracotta tiled roofs with white edges, overlapping in a wave pattern. In the old cottages, often as many as eleven tiny rooms were crammed into the ground floor. They were built with low ceilings so that less fuel was needed to warm them when firewood was scarce. Huddled low on the ground in the manner of Scottish crofters' houses, they are also less exposed to the gale force winds that sweep in from the sea.

New owners tend to change little of the houses, although they may decide to use the roof space for attic rooms, adding a dormer window to provide more light.

Often window seats, platforms, and storage units are built-in to save space.

Some of the homes in Skagen have large sheds attached for storing boats and fishing tackle, and walled terraces or courtyards that give shelter from the wind and sea. Weather vanes, in use when fishing boats were powered by sail, top many of the houses. The catch, brined and salted for the Danish *smorgasbord*, is pegged out to dry in the fading evening light.

1 *Seaside town of Skagen*
2 + 5 *Typical Skagen houses*
3 *Weather vane*
4 *Fish hanging out to dry*

2

3

4

5

LONG ISLAND CABIN

When *New York Times* reporter Suzanne Slesin and her husband, Michael Steinberg, take a break from the pressure of city life, they head for their small, one-storey house on Long Island. This 50-year-old property is situated in fashionable Bridgehampton, in an area of farmland that stretches to the ocean. It has an acre and a quarter of land and a pretty garden with wild pink roses.

The original structure was one of the farm outbuildings used to store tractors. Previous owners had redesigned the building as living quarters, and set two skylights in the shingle roof.

When Suzanne and Michael moved in, they exposed the rafters in the ceiling and added four sash windows along the back of the house to introduce a view of the garden. The ground floor is a sunny open-plan living area with wooden floors painted in grey deck paint. A screen door from the garden leads in to the kitchen, where china and ornaments are neatly displayed on track shelving. Nothing jars in the casual, comfortable atmosphere of this seaside house that is furnished with the timeless appeal of wicker and chintz.

1 *House and front garden*
2 *Living area*
3 *Kitchen/dining area*

3

LONG ISLAND BEACH HOUSE

A feature of the seaside is the extreme and rapidly changing weather, and houses on the coast have to be particularly resilient to withstand it. In the past such houses were often either weatherboarded, covered with shingle cladding, or tarred with pitch which acted as a protective seal.

One of the benefits of modern building and insulation materials is that they make redundant these messy and rather unsightly practices. Nowadays, houses can be opened up to reveal a view and introduce more light, without being exposed to the elements.

This house on Long Island was unlived in for some time, and in need of renovation when Bob and Joan Bayley discovered it. Although tarred and shingled, it had taken a battering from the wind, rain and sea spray. On inspection it was found to have a leaky roof and floorboards saturated with salt water. In spite of the damage, the Bayleys were captivated by the wooded site, with its magnificent views across the Atlantic, and they saw that the house had great potential.

The original structure was a one-room playhouse, built at the turn of the century and later used, in the 1930s, as a beach house. When tiny windows were put in to reduce draughts and prevent too much heat from escaping, the best sea views were lost as a result. Once the Bayleys had repaired the roof and insulated the house, they decided to open it out to extend the view of the bay. In the old playroom, they removed the wall and windows, and replaced them with sliding double-glazed doors. They added a semi-circular wooden terrace, like a ship's deck, that faces the sea, and is reached through sliding doors from the living room. East-facing rooms were also given large windows, and the cedar-panelled walls were painted white to reflect the daylight that floods into the house.

During summer months, meals are taken outside on the terrace; the indoor dining area is kept for use in the winter, when the family visit the house less often. An addition to the galley kitchen is a timber-frame conservatory, which is used as a summer living room. Some of the 1930s windows from the playroom have been used here, stacked up and fitted from floor to ceiling to maximize the amount of light that enters the room. The glazed roof has been hung with striped canvas blinds, which can be drawn back to introduce more light or pulled down to shade the room from the hot sun. A cement block floor is covered with a timber platform which simply lifts off like an old-fashioned slatted bath mat for cleaning. When

3

the weather turns cold, the unheated conservatory is simply sealed off from the kitchen with transparent plastic screens.

Two heating systems were installed in the house – electric panels on night storage for the upstairs bedrooms, and a double fireplace on either side of the chimney breast, which was built using stones from the beach. One fireplace burns logs, the other houses a pot-bellied range that radiates a steady heat.

The house is full of the owners' special collections of coloured bottles, old-fashioned toys, and various fish ornaments. In the kitchen, an illustration of two fishes makes an unusual splashback

behind the sink. A long narrow window provides a fine view, framed like another picture, of the trees that surround the house.

The bathroom, with its beachcomber collection of seashells (displayed on an old sash window), a starfish and some cobalt blue bottles, evokes sand and sea. The tones and textures of bleached wood and white matchboarding, hung with straw and Panama hats, are redolent of hazy days spent on the beach.

1 *Approach to the house*
2 *Summer living room*
3 *View from the kitchen window*
4 *Bathroom*

4

1

2

AEGEAN VILLA

The quest for a dream house became an obsession for the owner of this villa on the Greek island of Hydra. She first saw the island in 1955, by the light of a full moon and, from that moment, it was engraved upon her memory. Her dream was realized when she bought the 250-year-old house, perched on a hill above the Aegean.

Resting beneath a sea of dried vine leaves and faded bougainvillaea blossoms, the building was abandoned and in a state of disrepair. There were holes in the wooden floorboards, and peeling walls; inside, rainwater had collected in puddles, because the roof had leaked. But the scent of thyme and honey in the air, and the church bells ringing out across the valley convinced the purchaser that this was where she wanted to reside.

From the 100-year-old cypress tree that stands sentinel at the entrance to the house, 136 stone and wooden steps lead to the terraces, where Mediterranean plants flourish in the dry stone walls.

From one of the terraces you can see the town of Hydra and, in the distance, the island of Dokos.

The cool interior of the villa is plainly decorated. Large, dark wooden beams run the length of the rooms, and the thick white-washed walls are unadorned, except for the original built-in wooden cupboards, and brackets for candles. The only pattern is on the large terracotta floor tiles in the kitchen. Antique furniture, mostly found on the island, is solid and plain. A corner fireplace with a hooded chimney breast is typically Greek, and table and chairs are set close to it in the style of a country kitchen. On the hearth are some objects – bronze scales, a candlesnuff, a flat iron and a kettle – that are both functional and decorative, in tune with the monastic architecture. The atmosphere of calm that pervades the house, invites relaxation and peaceful contemplation.

1 *A view from the house*
2 *Dining area and hearth*
3 *Traditional wooden furniture*

1

VICTORIAN BOATHOUSES

The owners' brief to the architect, for a weekend retreat at Portsea in the Australian state of Victoria, was simple: all they requested was 'ordered informality'. Bearing this in mind, Graeme Gunn took his inspiration from a pair of Victorian boathouses on stilts in the shallows of the Pacific Ocean. The two small buildings, with their white weatherboarding and blue painted roofs had withstood the tides and the test of time – a fine example on which to base a modern beach house.

Gunn found the perfect site for the house, perched above the spectacular bay of white sand, like icing sugar. He sketched out the façade for the new house, pitching the roof at the same angle as that of the boathouses and defining the gables with white-painted trellis. He added a third pavilion to the line-up, and gave each one a clearly defined living area. The main bedroom on the left and the living room on the right, are linked by an informal glass-roofed dining area in the centre. All three have plastered dividing walls and doors that lead from one to another. Glass doors open onto the terrace where there is a swimming pool.

The inside is airy and orderly, with well-proportioned rooms. Although the building was inspired by Victorian architecture, it is essentially a modern interpretation, and modern furniture and fittings are perfectly at home here. So often, the flotsam and jetsam of another life washes into a second home, but it is refreshing to find that elegant modern decorations and designs have been chosen for this house.

The colour scheme is duotone white and ivory, grey and flint. These shell and oyster shades change subtly in different lights. The ceilings are constructed of timber and the walls are plaster or board. A touch of Victorian formality is retained in the high vaulted ceiling and marble-floored entrance hall. The transition from outdoors to indoors is softened by light filtering through the white trellis work of the pavilions and the terrace that runs the length of the bedroom and dining area.

An area of fragrant pine trees behind the house provides a perfect wooded backdrop; at the front, the lawn sweeps down to the beach. This is a holiday playhouse, playfully and simply executed, that evokes endless summer days of cricket, croquet, swimming and boating.

1 *Pavilions designed by Graeme Gunn*
2 *Victorian boathouses on the Pacific*

BALINESE JUNGLE RETREAT

A holiday home in Bali, Indonesia, may be as far from your budget as your shores, yet it has tremendous appeal for anyone seeking an exotic location. However, in order to build the perfect refuge on a tropical island you need help from a knowledgeable source (as Robinson Crusoe soon discovered). Dutch architect, Henk Vos, learned much from the local people, and adapted their traditional architecture, craft and building materials to produce this beautiful island house. His inspiration was the hut dwellings of the local inhabitants, with their bamboo and thatched roofs and mud walls.

Most holidaymakers in Bali inhabit the residential area for Westerners known as Batu Jimbar. The fishermen live along the seashore in huts on stilts, encircled by the palm trees that are part of their

1 *Thatched seating pavilion*
2 *Oriental lily pond and forest backdrop*

2

3

livelihood. Further inland, where the jungle gets denser and the soil is fertile, it is customary to build a series of huts or pavilions contained within a mud wall that keeps the jungle at bay.

Henk Vos has followed this principle for the house and outbuildings that he designed on a square plot of land at Batu Jimbar. Along the perimeter wall are tropical fruit trees, such as banana, papaya, breadfruit and coconut. The property is approached along a rustic brick path that leads to the many open pavilions, or *balés*. These make up the main building of guest house, living quarters and work area, each with its own separate bathroom. Nearby is the *metén* (master bedroom), which is a separate brick and stone pavilion with two beds.

Instead of using the traditional sunbaked and hand-smoothed mud floors for the pavilions, Vos has specified white ceramic tiles, which are cool underfoot. White brick platforms, built around low tables, create simple seating, covered with cushions and bolsters in slub-weave Thai silk.

All the buildings have conical bamboo and thatch roofs supported by narrow columns that are strong enough to withstand fifty seasons of monsoon squalls. Roof beams are lashed and pegged together, using a traditional building technique that requires no nails. Then grass, about 18 inches (45 cm) thick, is laid on this lattice of bamboo. Once on the wooden support frame, the thatch is combed down to the eaves and trimmed with a sickle.

Although the structure of the building is simple, and the furnishing discreet, certain features give the house character. There is an ancient Balinese door, carved by local craftsmen, in the main pavilion. This is set in plaster relief work. There are cornices and skirting boards defining the inner space, wood carvings decorating the walls in the bedroom; and various glazed pots and Balinese stone sculptures throughout the house. The only touches of colour in a neutral scheme are the bright cushions and bolsters on the seating platforms, and the brightly coloured flowers from the garden.

The architect's intention was to leave views unobstructed. The low eaves of the conical roof protect the occupants from the weather, offering shade in the heat and shelter from the rain, so there is no need for panes of glass. For privacy, the full-length rattan blinds can be let down over the entrances.

In the garden, the owners have turned a sunken Japanese trench – a relic of World War II – into an oriental lily pond, crossed by wooden platforms and stone slabs. The waterside pavilion provides an ideal place for peaceful reflection in a prolific garden of scented flowers. At night, brass or stone pots are filled with water fragrant with floating frangipani flowers. In such an idyllic setting, the customs of the Far East are observed as much for their ritual significance as for the pleasures of reclining by the pond, or looking out at the sparkling sea beyond.

4

3 *Sitting area with garden view*
4 *Balinese carved doorway*
5 *Ornamental pool*

5

CORNISH SEAFRONT STUDIO

Strong surf, fine sands and giddy skies make Cornwall a favourite holiday haunt in England. In this south-western part of the country, the tides ebb and flow for astonishing distances, leaving ribs of sand that glisten with water, and tide pools for shrimping. Since the sea can be tempestuous, every seaside town and village is protected by a sea wall.

St Ives is a small harbour town on the north coast of Cornwall, known for its artistic community of painters, sculptors and potters. The sea wall, which was built in 1801 to stop sand blown from Porthmeor beach from choking the harbour, is lined with grey stone cottages that were once sail lofts and fish cellars for the fleet. One of these cottages is owned by photographer Ron Sutherland, who has converted it to a studio for working and holidaying.

According to ordnance

1 *Sea front at St Ives*

1

2

survey maps, the cottage was probably built in 1877. When Ron Sutherland discovered it, the roof had fallen in and the skylight was broken, so that salt spray and rain water were spilling over into buckets below. The cellar of the next-door building (a store for nets and crab pots) ran up to his house, but on a slightly higher level than the ground floor, thereby creating a draught. An architect friend, Maxim Benthall, produced a grand plan for the house that included a large window running the length of the house, with a balcony overhanging the beach. This idea was rejected by the local planning committee, so instead he designed a 17-foot window that provides an uninterrupted view of the beach and the Atlantic. It comprises a series of panels, each with a sealed double-glazed unit, that can withstand storm force gales. One panel is a door onto the beach, although you need a ladder to climb down to the sand below. The cottage façade, opened up by this window, is so close to the sea that the owner can observe its changes of mood, from the shelter of his living room.

Protecting the cottage from the sea and weather was not easy, and involved the laborious task of making the thick walls watertight. Old oak ships' masts had been built in as door lintels, but they were discovered to be sodden and had to be replaced, together with some rotten floorboards. The new floorboards were dried in a kiln so that they wouldn't shrink. Stable doors were retained, and the top half of the front door was glazed so that light can filter in.

Open-plan living was considered the answer in this tiny, narrow cottage. The kitchen and living area make up the ground floor, with a lean-to bathroom at the back; upstairs there is an open, sparsely furnished bedroom. The staircase is blocked in with a pillar construction, like a beach hut, that houses an understairs cupboard and built-in oven. A clever *trompe l'oeil* effect is gained with the glass oven door that reflects the sea and sky outside.   3

4

Pale grey walls and white gloss timber, together with the large glass panels, add to the general airiness of the studio. The floors – an inky blue colour like the sea – give the rooms visual depth. With such a strong colour underfoot, it was important to introduce contrast colours of equal intensity. Broad deck-chair green and white stripes were chosen for the sofa and chairs, while the cover on the bed upstairs is blue with a narrow white stripe. The whole house is warmed by a black cast-iron gas stove, which has a large industrial flue extending through the window well to the upstairs.

As photographers are particularly sensitive to changes in the light, the owner has installed recessed track lighting on the ceiling and overhead lights on dimmer switches, so that he can control the intensity of light inside as the daylight starts to fade.

Designed around the sea and sands, this beach house has a natural affinity with its surroundings. The proximity of the seashore is reflected inside by the deck-chair colours and the seagull mobile hanging from the rafters, the owner's enthusiasms by the fishing rods at the door and the surfboards propped against the wall, ready for use.

2 *Living room*
3 *Upstairs bedroom*
4 *Stair cupboard with oven*

1

2

3

MANGO BAY, BARBADOS

There can be few settings as dramatic as an island in the West Indies, and no place more appropriate for set designer Oliver Messel to design his dream house. Although he was not a qualified architect, he had an encyclopaedic knowledge of architecture, a lifelong interest in interior design and a great love for the mild tropical climate of the Caribbean.

He longed to build a house for himself in Barbados, and he eventually found the perfect site, close to the popular Sandy Lane Hotel. Governed by traditional laws of inheritance, the land was divided into tiny plots and he had to negotiate with 50 owners before he could purchase it. Ironically, the house he had planned for himself was eventually designed as a holiday home for Mr and Mrs Aall, who periodically visited Barbados and wanted a property there.

This two-storey house, called Mango Bay because of the fine mango tree in the garden, was designed in 1968 and completed the following year. Modelled on the grand old estate houses, it is settled in its luxuriant surroundings as if it were a century old, an impression enhanced by the traditional features of pillared loggia, louvred green shutters and outside staircase, and the use of local coral stone. The garden, with a lawn that stretches to the sea, has old mahogany, tamarisk and cordia trees, and an African tulip in the front drive. A bridge, in the oriental style, spans the swimming pool.

Messel incorporated a design feature for which he became renowned – a vista from the front facade, through the house, to the caribbean sea beyond. An open loggia runs the length and width of the ground floor and frames a magnificent view. The room is decorated in the fine blue and white colours of china, with chair covers in the same oriental pattern, and framed blue and white chinoiserie tiles. A Chinese porcelain elephant and lion, more Pekinese than African, stand guard upon the pink and white terrazzo floor.

Oliver Messel's designs for the theatre, ballet, opera and cinema were praised for their delicate, magical quality. His unconventional talent found expression in the tropical islands of the Caribbean, and nowhere is this more apparent than at Mango Bay. Although the furnishing of the house is different today, many examples of Messel's original style remain, in decorative features such as the carved monkey chandelier and flower spray lamps.

1 *Mango Bay, surrounded by luxuriant foliage*
2 *Loggia*
3 *Bridge over the pool*

DECK HOUSE ON THE PACIFIC

Peter McIntyre, an architect who sails an ocean racing boat, built this family holiday home on a peninsula outside Melbourne in Australia. Although the area is exposed to strong prevailing winds, the house is sited in a negative air pocket created by the breeze rushing up the cliff face, and is therefore sheltered.

The McIntyre family camped for months on the clifftop so that they could analyse the weather patterns, before deciding on the best position for their house. As there are three architects in the family, the design of the building, and the materials used to build it, were a matter for lengthy discussion. The corrugated iron roof, an indigenous feature of Australian buildings, is held down with steel cables that run through the timber frame and are fixed to the stumps. A yachting interest is apparent in the way that the house is tuned, ship-like, to the weather. It is arranged in several layers, with screens and glazed panels that slide on

and off the building like sails. The inner core is a stone-clad fireplace, the second layer is a veranda that can be enclosed, and the third is an open deck. Panels at the front and back of the veranda will slide away to open up the house to the cool sea breezes.

Open decks surround the house, with steps down to the very edge of the cliff. On one circular platform, the family set up pillows and an Italian market umbrella when the weather is good. The interior space is a large living area with couches, window seats and day beds. Open decks can be used for sleeping too. Natural wood and vertical cedar boards, used both inside and out, are bleached to give a timeless, weather-beaten quality.

The McIntyres' house shows an appreciation of nature in all its aspects. Even the access road to the front door was hand cut, rather than bulldozed, in the interest of land conservation.

1 Sundeck
2 Kitchen/diner
3 Inner deck overlooking the Pacific

2

3

1

2

FISHERMAN'S COTTAGE IN IRELAND

A love of the wild sea and shingled shoreline brought Fergus Flynn-Rogers to this tiny cottage, one of five remaining of an old fishing community in County Louth. He discovered the two-roomed cottage in 1965, when he was an architectural student in Dublin, and bought it for just thirty six pounds.

His main objective was to create a room full of light, but still preserve the two-roomed space, so he built a frame to sit on the original masonry and screwed plate glass to it.

The cottage is full of Fergus Flynn-Rogers' innovations: he converted the pigsty to a bathroom, built the four-poster bed, which can be used as a bunk bed, and created a sleeping loft on a mezzanine floor in the living room. It is now warm and cosy on winter evenings, with a fire that burns driftwood from the beach.

1 *Fisherman's cottage*
2 *Kitchen*
3 *Living room*

3

1

2

AUSTRALIAN COASTAL RETREAT

On the remote and barren south coast of New South Wales, Australia, this building shimmers in the pink dawn like some extra-terrestrial spacecraft. Clad in silver corrugated iron that picks up the light, with louvred windows set in aluminium frames, the low lines and sweeping roof give the building a luminous appearance. Yet the architect, Glenn Murcett, has used traditional Australian building materials for this unusual seaside house. The galvanized iron on the outside is a material used for roofs throughout the country, from Federal State buildings to sheep-shearing stations.

The house overlooks a lake on one side, the Pacific Ocean on the other; to the west is a distant view of mountains. In this southern hemisphere it is the northern aspect of the house that gets the best light and warmth in winter. The owners, who enjoy quiet hobbies such as reading and sewing, often come here to relax in the winter sunlight.

The purposeful design responds to sunlight and shade to produce a building in harmony with the sparse and open land upon which it stands. The impression of the building from a distance is of a long shed, as uncomplicated as an aircraft hangar. But once inside, the sophisticated design is revealed.

The owners wanted a house that would give a feeling of being outside when inside, was close to the elements, yet protected from them, and easy to maintain. It was built in two self-contained sections so that they, and their four grown-up children, could have separate living areas within the same house. The two wings are linked, from east to west, by an inner courtyard. Following the roof line, you can see the broad curve over the living rooms and the smaller curve that houses the bathrooms and kitchens. The parents' wing contains a kitchen, sitting and dining area with fireplace, a bedroom and shower. The children's wing has a living room, kitchen with pot-bellied stove, dining area and two bedrooms, each containing single beds and built-in cupboards. A separate shower and laundry room can be used when friends come to stay.

The colour scheme throughout the house is grey, cream and white, and furnishing is minimal so that the owners have no worries about the house and its contents when they're away. The wooden furniture is functional, and resilient to the wear and tear of young people and holiday living.

1 + 2 *Exterior, seen from the west*
3 *Living rooms joined by an open court*

1

2

MEDITERRANEAN VILLA

The colours of sea, sand and sky are contained in this bright villa on the south coast of France. Perched above the Mediterranean at Sète, with a view of the gulf and the Bouzique oyster beds, it has been transformed from a humble fisherman's shack to a holiday house. Designed by painter and architect Gilles Dupuy, the open, arched views and bold decoration celebrate the clear light of the south of France. Building extensions open out from the central shack, like wings, one housing a bathroom and two bedrooms, the other a spacious living room and kitchen, linked by a courtyard.

Giant arches, like viaducts, allow the sunlight to stream into the lofty rooms. A vaulted ceiling soars above, washed in blue to blur the distinction between inside and out, ceiling and sky. On a more practical note, the tradition of painting interiors blue to repel winged insects is used here, as it was by Van Gogh in his room at Arles. Splashes of sunshine yellow and Provençal printed material decorate the airy living room and, as dusk falls, these colours echo the lavender of the hillsides and the regional lemon groves.

The skirting boards and wooden beams in the vaulted ceiling are defined in a deeper blue to accentuate the fine proportions of the room. A cool tiled floor, the pattern as ornate as a mosaic, is laid with small and large tiles.

The intention was to free the villa of too much clutter. Furniture is a mixture of period and modern, united by its simple lines and neutral colours. Bolsters covered in pillow slips and tied with ribbon make attractive supports on sofas and beds.

In the dining area, over-looking the Gulf of Lions, the colourful table is set with hand-painted earthenware dishes. Protected from the weather by sliding glass panels, this is a pleasant place to relax, especially when the mistral blows in from the north.

1 *Arched sitting room*
2 *Table overlooking the terrace and Gulf of Lions*
3 *Sitting/dining area*

3

1

FEDERAL STYLE IN AUSTRALIA

A charming seaside house with a mature garden is lovingly maintained on the Bellarine Peninsula in the state of Victoria, Australia. Although it resembles the gracious white weatherboard houses of New England, with their sweeping lawns, it is in fact a building in the unique Australian architectural style, known as Federal, which became popular around the turn of the century when the nine states were joined in federation. Built in 1890, the house has not always been a grand symbol of an elegant age. Unsympathetic additions, by previous owners, had cloaked its original form and neglect left it uninhabitable. Dilapidated outhouses on either side ruined the once fine façade.

The present owners, who successfully bid for the house at a local auction, were far-sighted in their determination to restore it to its original splendour. Their renovation brought the house into the twentieth century with bathrooms en suite, and a modern kitchen. Inside, the original high ceilings, so essential for the circulation of sea breezes, had been covered with plasterboard. These were revealed again and air circulation is now assisted by fans set in the ceiling. Some of the partition walls in the smaller, darker rooms were knocked down to give more space. Attic rooms within the high-pitched roof were transformed into rooms for the children, and window seats, skirted with fabric, were built into alcoves to provide places to sit and look out at the garden and the sea.

Signs of indoor and outdoor pursuits are revealed in the entrance hall where books, tennis rackets, wind breaks, straw hats and sun visors are stored side by side. A hand-made Australian pine table, displaying flowers from the garden, a wicker chair, and a rag rug are simple furnishings for a gracious entrance. The location of the house is

1 *Weatherboard house and front lawn*
2 *Jetty adjoining the property*
3 *Corner of entrance hall*

2

3

4

5

perfectly suited to the owners' love of the outdoors, with a jetty tacked onto the property for fishing. The established garden, which is an unusual feature for a seaside house, has been well tended. Shrubs and fine lawns are irrigated by the natural spring water found close to the surface of the site – a discovery of great importance to a gardener in a hot climate, where fresh water is often hard to find. A local gardener looks after the grounds during the week, until the owners return to replenish the terracotta pots with seasonal flowers. These look welcoming on the steps that lead to the veranda and the cool interior.

The house has been furnished simply with some period pieces that have no great value, but a dignity that has stood the test of time. There is an old wooden dining table from Rugby school in England, wicker furniture, and comfortable easy chairs covered in white Indian cotton. A French elm bench serves as a coffee table in the living room, doubling up for extra seating.

In the kitchen a Mexican plate rack displays a collection of hand-painted plates, decorated with birds, boats and fishing scenes. All the storage space is open, with a central island dividing the long rectangular room. Against a cream background, the blinds, shelves and stools are in the traditional blue green of New England country kitchens, known as a milk can colour because it was used to decorate them. Here, the only reminder of modern living is the breakfast bar with hob and pull-up stools.

Mellow golden wood was preferred, by the owners, to the local dark hardwood – jarrah – which is indigenous to Australia. Old pine floorboards were sanded and polished, and sealed with matt varnish. The unpretentious charm of the decorative scheme can be seen in the freshness and simplicity of the furnishings, such as the rag rugs collected in South Carolina, the American folk art, baskets of dried flowers and framed children's drawings.

4 *Mexican plate rack*
5 *Sitting room*
6 *Kitchen*

CHAPTER THREE

MOUNTAINSIDE

When you head for the hills and mountain slopes, you set out to escape from it all. As you climb higher, the air becomes fresher and more invigorating, and the light has a luminous clarity. Mountaineers and skiers are familiar with the peaceful silence of the mountains, which have always had a solitary appeal. Hermits take sanctuary there, and climbers are lured upwards by the beauty and mystery of the heights.

With its backdrop of awesome mountain peaks, the terrain is more challenging than any other location. For those who hanker after healthy outdoor pursuits rather than cosy rural activities, mountain areas are unsurpassed in natural facilities. Holidaymakers come here to enjoy winter sports and activities such as hiking, mountaineering, skiing and sledging. Even in summer, when the slopes are carpeted with grass and Alpine flowers, and streams flow with melted snow, mountainside holidays have an air of adventure. There are also some mountain areas that offer a different world from that of snowcapped peaks and ski slopes, and enjoy a warmer climate too. The Andalusian range of southern Spain, for example, the rugged terrain of a Greek island, or the foothills of the Himalayas have much to recommend them.

You will pay a price for the unspoilt beauty and seclusion of a mountainous region: it is less likely to be served by a major airport, and if you travel by road you may be hampered by snow and ice. You will be limited in your choice of holiday home too, since mountain properties are less numerous than those by the sea or in the country. They are often in areas that are underdeveloped, because of the difficult terrain and lack of industry. The buildings themselves have often been subjected to the extreme climate, with their roofs taking most of the strain from heavy snowfall and high winds. The cost of restoring an old building in the mountains is therefore very high.

Designing buildings for these breathtaking sites is not easy. Granite blocks and slate tiles, glacial stones and indigenous timbers have been employed in shepherd's huts, barns and outhouses, chalets and lodges. Sometimes old mountain crafts, such as the drystone-walling technique, have been revived.

Previous page: Chalets near Gotzens, Austria

Resourcefulness is necessary for getting things to a site too; in the Alps a helicopter airlifted a new septic tank into a holiday home, because access was so difficult. Similarly, the British in India brought their Victorian claw-footed bathtubs to the hill-station houses at Simla on a steam train from Bombay, over 1000 miles away.

The elevations of the buildings in these regions are often inspired by the rugged mountain ranges that surround them. They are constructed on a vertical line with peaked roofs and crag-like gables, and balconies that act as viewing platforms. Rarely one-storey houses, they span different levels and approaches, with stairs a particular feature both inside and out. Even the traditional chalets in the valleys have basements that raise the living areas above the heavy snowdrifts, and haylofts reached by outside stairs. In Finland, where the snowfall is very heavy, the roofs of houses have a network of small ladders, which allows the snow sweeper to make his ascent. In Tibet, it is again the climate that dictates the design of the mountainside buildings. The houses have a sunken granary in the flat roof, reached by a ladder, and here the farmers ferment an alcoholic muesli to nourish the family through nine months of snow.

In high altitudes, the open fire tends to be the core of the house and, in this chapter, you will find many homes where open-plan living is designed around the fireplace so that each area benefits from its warmth. The austerity of the mountains is tempered inside the houses with soft, natural furnishings in fleece, down and hide. Warm, vibrant colours are used to counterbalance the coldness of the environment. Even in modern resorts, dining areas and extra guest rooms are considered in the design: in a Vermont ski lodge, space is trimmed from the kitchen to enlarge the living area, while in an Australian resort, window seats double up as platform beds for visitors. Furniture is solid — handcarved cupboards, chests and dressers — as anything spindly or elaborate would be inappropriate in such a setting. Thick carpets or rugs underfoot provide extra warmth in cold climates, and soothe tired feet freed from skis and climbing boots.

Norwegian ski lodge

Many mountain resorts offer rented accommodation for the season and then close the entire development in summer months for financial reasons. If you want a base for skiing holidays, consider a scheme whereby you lease a chalet or apartment for the skiing season, which is then let to other holidaymakers in milder weather.

Mountain areas are excellent holiday spots in all seasons, with spectacular scenery and a range of outdoor pursuits. Resorts such as Aspen in the Rocky Mountains, St Moritz in Switzerland and the Snowy Mountains of Australia, are lively all year round for shooting the rapids, pony trekking, rock climbing and walking.

In mountainside areas, where mist, frost and snow are regular visitors, the houses require careful, and often expensive, maintenance. Heating, services and supplies are so important in high altitudes that you should not consider buying a mountain property without fully investigating the cost and responsibility this entails. Access in winter months may involve purchasing or renting a reliable vehicle, equipped for blizzard conditions.

❄ The time-share schemes that are popular for beach resorts, are now attracting people to previously prohibitively expensive mountainside locations, such as the Scottish highlands. Time-sharing means you are buying the right to spend chosen periods every year in the same property for a specified number of years, or sometimes for life. You are not usually investing in property as such. Unscrupulous developers and gullible buyers can find themselves in complex legal wrangles that result from high-pressure sales techniques. Established in the United States for some time, it is becoming easier to sell your time-share investment there. Elsewhere you are likely to find it difficult to sell, since those attracted to the

scheme will want to buy into a brand new development, particularly since some properties have suffered serious depreciation and delapidation. Potential buyers are offered enticements to visit developments and the hard-sell often starts at airports. Once a deposit is paid it is seldom repaid if you change your mind. Never feel guilty about refusing a tempting offer, and never part with money without fully investigating what you are buying. Give yourself a chance to consider the deal over a period of time, while you obtain legal advice.

❄ An alternative to time-shares, particularly for those who want a mountain location and outdoor activities, includes taking shares in a company and acquiring a title deed, with club or country club membership. You can invest in a property company with properties all over the world, rather than taking a time-share in a particular property. This gives you flexibility for your holidays, and also an investment that is easy to resell.

MAINTENANCE

● The age of the property, the quality of the building and the climate it has to withstand are all key factors of maintenance. In a hot country seasonal maintenance will be different from in a cold climate where snow, frost and ice take their toll. Homes left unoccupied for long periods will deteriorate because you are not on hand to deal with problems. Be prepared to spend part of your holiday period organizing repairs. If you do not visit the place regularly, pay someone to check your property at regular intervals so that they can inform you of damage and organize essential repairs in your absence. Make these general checks when you first inspect the property and during each visit.
● Before you go inside the house, look at the state of brick, stone or wood cladding. Take some binoculars so that you can look at the roof.
● Check the distance of trees from the house. Some large trees have tenacious roots which can undermine the foundations of the house.
● Blocked gutters and chimney flues, cracked pipes, broken or missing roof tiles and faulty chimney flashings cause damp. Inside, you may be able to see or smell damp, which spots the inside of cupboards, round skirting boards or stains walls.
● Seasonal maintenance of the roof, chimney, gutters and drains is important, so check them before winter sets in.
● A quarter of the heat lost from a house is through the roof, so make sure it is insulated. Double-glazed windows will also prevent heat loss in winter. Adequate ventilation is also important when you are insulating a house.
● Whatever heating system you use, keep adequate fuel supplies, and make sure that access is possible for deliveries.
● The garden will require maintenance too. If you are not a keen gardener, plan and plant one that is easy to care for.

1

2

SKI LODGE IN VERMONT

When the sky is blue and the snow deep and inviting, skiers want to be out on the slopes, not huddled indoors. The newest apartments in a ski resort on the Sachem trail in Vermont have been designed around the leisure activities that are so much part of a skiing holiday. The first fifty houses in the scheme, opened ten years ago, were solid family houses that needed too much maintenance and heating, so real estate owners in Connecticut commissioned architect Zane Yost to design a hundred apartments that would fit in with the changing needs of the holiday market.

His prototype floor plan can be adapted to four different designs, depending on the size required.

Set amongst the silver birches, these matchboarded houses are self-contained units with a large fireside living area. An outdoor sundeck, with a roof of plexiglass, takes in the sun all year round, and sheds snow easily. Inside, the roof elevation houses some loft bedrooms, and skylights have been set in the high-pitched ceiling to improve the light in these upstairs rooms.

The interior scheme considers the skier's particular needs, providing more closet space for bulky clothing and equipment, and wall-to-wall carpet that is warm underfoot

when boots are unclipped. Walls are painted in warm cream, with cushions and wall-hangings in soft fireglow colours. Windows are triple-glazed to cut heat loss, the fireplace doors cut out draughts, and the ceiling fan, usually associated with houses in hot climates, circulates hot air generated by off-peak electric panels. Since *après ski* is more important than cooking, kitchens are small. The basement area, which is self-contained, has a laundry, additional sleeping quarters and direct access to the outside.

---

1 *Exterior with silver birches*
2 *Open-plan living area*

1

2

ADOBE HOUSE IN NEW MEXICO

This adobe house in Santa Fe, state capital of New Mexico, looks more like part of a film set than a holiday home. Built in 1920 in the style of the Mexican Indian *pueblos*, it nestles in the foothills of the Rockies, at a height of about 6,000 feet. The warmth of the midday sun is held in the clay walls long after dusk, and the solar energy panels along the perimeter wall harness additional heat.

Lynne and Donnell Moore discovered the house in the quiet Barrio quarter, the oldest part of Santa Fe. The building shares the same cultural heritage as the town – a blend of Spanish and Mexican Indian. The ranch-style furniture includes tubbed leather seats, like saddles, that are set on wicker bases, and carved wooden tables. Floors are constructed of cream flagstones, and rough-hewn beams support the roof above cream painted walls.

Originally a small hut, its extensions have occurred easily and sympathetically. In 1980, architect Robert Peter added new wings to the . . original building, so that now there is a large living area on a site of about 600 square metres (about ⅙th acre). Familiar with the communal settlements of New Mexico, he knew that clay walls hold the warmth of the sun, so he built long *bancos*, or benches, of clay along the terrace walls, lining them with canvas seating that can be rolled up. He also built solar panels into the walls, at intervals, to store the heat in the space between.

In the hacienda tradition, he placed chimneys at all four corners of the house so that every indoor and outdoor area has a corner fireplace. On wintry nights, fires are lit in all the rooms and heat radiates in a fan shape. On the patio, the open fire glows in the corner and provides warmth for those sitting out in the cool of the evening.

1 *Walled terrace and corner fireplace*
2 *Interior*

2

SHEPHERD'S HUT IN SWITZERLAND

A shepherd's stone shelter, near Lake Lugano on the Swiss/Italian border, was once a single windowless room with a sheep pen and a fireplace. Today, it houses a spacious open-hearthed living room, and a basement that is still used as sleeping quarters.

The descent to the hut is along a precipitous donkey path, so when renovations on the property began it proved cheaper to airlift the cesspit by helicopter, onto the site, rather than bring it down the mountainside. In the summer when Alpine flowers and grasses carpet the slopes the owner, Ruth Fehr, reaches the hut easily, but in heavy snow the climb takes half an hour. A teacher well versed in timetables, she makes the journey from Zurich across Lake Lugano to her 'stable with the well worn face' each weekend, even if she can only stay for five hours.

The plot is just under one acre, fronted by conifers and an Alpine meadow. Two springs emerge nearby, and one provides drinking water which is piped into the house. The roof of clinker tiles, as variegated in colour as the stones that line the glacial valley, has been newly secured on five chestnut posts to withstand snowdrifts and icy winds. Original air vents have been balanced with windows secured by solid wooden shutters that won't rattle on a stormy night.

At such a high altitude heating is of the utmost importance, so the architect, Markus Wespi, designed a fireplace that would warm the whole room, with cushioned seats covered in cow hide set around the hearth. A seating platform can be turned into an extra bed, and a built-in headrest positioned so that Ruth Fehr can see through the window to the cherry tree that flowers in spring.

Materials used throughout the house are local stone, slabbed for the central hearth; and felled timber of the region. Red ochre has been built into the back wall of the fireplace so that there is a warm glow even when it is unlit. In the kitchen there are slate worktops, set low at the owner's request, and a fireplace with a brick-built oven for the pizzas and tarts that are her speciality. The dining table will seat nine people. From here they can see the sheep grazing on the slope and, in the distance, Monte Caprino.

For years Ruth Fehr dreamt of finding a peaceful retreat in the mountains that would be easy to maintain. Now that her dream has come true, she is happy to make the pilgrimage to her second home every week.

1 *Stone hut on the mountain slope*
2 *Kitchen and dining area*

HIMALAYAN HILL STATION

In the days of the Raj, when the British ruled India, it became fashionable to head for the fresher air of the hills as summer approached. In 1864 the Viceroy, John Lawrence, declared Simla to be the summer capital, and it was here that the British built their pseudo-Tudor mansions and bungalows, nestling between the tennis courts and golf courses. Today, some are maintained as clubs, others have been transformed into hotels and *dak* bungalows. The interiors are pure Victoriana: bathrooms with glossy painted surfaces, and cool, high-ceilinged bedrooms with furniture made by local craftsmen. Given the pattern books of Europe to copy, they interpreted unfamiliar styles with a certain individuality. Brass, rattan, and Arts and Crafts wallpaper, all have the timeless quality that India imparts to visitors.

1 *View of the Himalayas*
2 + 3 *Bathroom & bedroom*

1

2

3

1

ALPINE CHALET

The most popular ski resort in France is the Val d'Isère in the Savoie region of the Alps. The ski slopes and facilities are much praised, but the architecture, which consists mainly of modern A-frame chalets and large holiday complexes, is seldom admired. Yet in an unspoilt hamlet called Fornet, the restoration of old barns and outhouses is transforming the mountainside.

In the patchy spring snow, just three kilometres from Val d'Isère, these stone houses blend in with their Alpine surroundings. The architect, André Laurenti, rebuilt twenty of them, using local craftsmen to build drystone walls and clinker tiled roofs in the traditional style of the region. He also redesigned the interiors, equipping the chalets with heating, a laundry, and all modern comforts. Walls were raised one metre to create more space inside, and the simple barn door and windows were replaced with cherry wood frames and glass panels.

This four-bedroomed chalet, once an old sheep pen, is now used for family holidays. The living room, kitchen and study are on one floor, and there is a basement utility area that houses the boilers, and skis on storage racks. The centrepiece of the living room is a stone fireplace, with a wooden slatted chimney hood above the hearth. There are no rugs or carpets on the blue stone floor, but the rooms are filled with large furniture – carved wooden cupboards, and fruitwood benches and marriage chests. There are dressers of larch and walnut, and antique patchworks on the wall.

Whereas in a seaside house the natural theme is fish, shells and ships, in mountain homes the decorative accessories tend to include craftwork from mountainous regions. In this holiday home, a woollen shepherd's cloth, fleecy blankets and woven shawls cover the rough plastered walls.

1 Stone chalet
2 Living room
3 Carved wooden furniture

2

3

AUSTRALIAN SKI RESORT

A new Australian ski resort called Dinner Plain stands 5,200 feet above sea level, just ten minutes drive on a shuttle service from Mount Hotham, the highest resort in Australia. The first snow falls here, and lingers longer than elsewhere. On a recreation area of 570 acres, it is the gateway to the high plains for cross-country skiers and, in summer, bushwalkers, fishermen and riders.

The building project began eight years ago, when Melbourne architect Peter McIntyre laid on the essential services for the condominiums, houses and a 40-bedroomed lodge. Each dwelling is connected to water, sewage and heating systems and has clear road access in heavy snows. Within McIntyre's basic design there are as many

1 *Exterior, Seadog House*
2 *Drying room, Seadog House*
3 *Living area, Seadog House*

configurations as there are market preferences. Exteriors follow the pattern of vertical or horizontal lapped-cedar boards, all weathered to the subtle grey-green colour of the eucalyptus trees that dot the landscape. The roof of corrugated iron, on straight joists that show as over-sized beams inside, has twisted springing points that follow the swoop of a plane wing on the outside. Like all well-designed houses in mountainous regions, roofs are built to shed snow easily.

The show house, Seadog House, has other classic ski-resort features: a protected area for logs, an area where skis can be removed, garage space, and a drying room for skis, shovels, sledges and warm clothing. The insulation is as basic as the skier's anorak: all houses have a frame of aluminium reflective foil casing, clad with timber and insulated with fibreglass.

The house is warm and cave-like, with a low hearth surrounded by fireside seats. A central wall, which divides the space diagonally, undulates to allow cross currents of warm air to circulate through two storeys to the bedrooms above. A partition wall projects from the kitchen to create a dining area. On the north side is a sundeck with built-in platform window seats that double-up as extra beds. Practical furnishing includes a natural hessian wall covering for extra warmth, brick-coloured carpets that don't show the dirt, and a colour scheme throughout in warm shades of red and orange, tempered with blue and charcoal. Another house, Steele House, features curved, horizontal and vertical windows.

Emotional functionalism is the philosophy that Peter McIntyre holds after 30 years in practice as an architect. He believes that the way you feel about a building is just as important as the architecture, if not more so. His functionalism can be detected in the architectural plans, but the emotional aspect, which is harder to define, is expressed in the soaring line of the roof, and a joyous celebration of the mountain peaks and slopes in the elevations of the houses.

4 *Steele House, part of the complex*

4

CHAPTER FOUR

WATERSIDE

Whether it is lakeside, riverside, or merely overlooking the village pond, a holiday home with a view across water is very desirable, and this is reflected in the price. This tranquil setting is the most sought after worldwide. Even within the same waterside development, apartments on the waterfront fetch up to 25 per cent more than those at the back of the building. There is a world of difference between a large house overlooking the upper reaches of the Thames and a tiny gîte beside a tributary of the Dordogne, but both will fetch a higher price than similar properties without the view. Extras, such as a jetty or private mooring for a boat, will also increase the value of a waterside property.

Lakelands all over the world attract those seeking a peaceful retreat. Britain's Lake District, the lakes of northern Italy, the great lakes of North America and those between France and Switzerland, and in the Scandinavian countries, offer established resorts. Developers of prime waterfront sites have built time-share apartments and holiday villas with adjacent marinas, shops and recreations, including boathouses, jetties, towpaths and banks for fishing. Unlike many coastal areas, these waterside sites are in harmony with their natural surroundings, and they are seldom deluged with boatloads of daytrippers. The sounds that disturb you at the waterside are more likely to be the chugging of the lake steamer, or the squeak of rowlocks, than the beat of the discotheque. Fishing, boating, bathing, or picnicking on the grassy banks of the river, are the peaceful pursuits of those who choose to holiday beside water.

The landscape is not easy to develop, so modern hotel complexes and apartment blocks are a rare sight. The climate will also deter holidaymakers who are looking for guaranteed sunshine. But for those who find that the French Riviera is beyond their reach, a beautiful waterside setting, a relaxed pace, and access to elegant and atmospheric old towns, is an attractive holiday alternative.

Since waterside sites are usually flat, they are ideal for the timber frame chalets popular in Scandinavia and North America. Variously described as

Previous page: Fishing huts, near Torsburg, Sweden

chalets, bungalows, or villas, they blend in with the waterside setting, whether it is a lake, loch or Irish lough. These wooden houses, that can be easily assembled on the site, are built around a timber frame, like old Tudor houses, but without the mortar cladding. They are light, warm and dry because less water is used in their construction than plastered cement houses – an important consideration in damp areas. Since there are no load bearing inner walls, the internal design of the houses can be altered to suit the buyers' needs.

Owners of waterside houses are well aware of the danger of flooding. Cynics say that in summer a riverside house has the river at the bottom of the garden while, in winter, the garden is at the bottom of the river. However, modern barrier control schemes have reduced the threat of flooding. Some older buildings that are ripe for conversion, such as millhouses or lock-keepers' sturdy cottages, are anchored on strong basements that will withstand such eventualities. Other traditional waterside houses – water towers and lakeside villas – were often tall and narrow to raise them high above the water level. Hoists and cranes would be used to lift furniture and other things to the top floor.

Taking to the water, rather than living beside it, means buying or hiring a boat. Maintaining a mooring can be dauntingly expensive, so it is essential to be totally committed to its upkeep. One idyllic holiday on a rented narrowboat, meandering down the canals through gentle countryside, does not prepare you for being a full-time houseboat owner. On the other hand, a houseboat offers nearly all the conveniences of a home on dry land. It can be sufficiently settled for a telephone line to be connected, with running water and electricity laid on, but the gangplank can easily be hoisted to give you the feeling of cutting loose. In this chapter you will find an architect-designed pontoon on the river Loire, a handcarved houseboat in Kashmir for travellers escaping the hot dusty Indian plains, and brightly painted narrowboats, once carriers of cargo on the canals, that have been converted into unconventional holiday homes.

SECURITY

Any building which is not permanently occupied is susceptible to thieves, trespassers, vandals and squatters.

- Do not leave anything in your holiday home which you consider irreplaceable, either sentimentally or financially.
- An insurance policy will cover the contents of your house. Questions asked by the company will help you to assess how secure your home is, as you must specify the number of doors, windows, locks and skylights, as well as how much time you spend there.
- Insurance must be increased by a considerable amount if you rent out the property.
- Good window bolts and door locks could be sufficient in a place where the neighbours are in residence, or a local person calls to check the property when it's empty. The more remote the property, the more difficult it will be to secure since burglars have the benefit of not being overlooked. You may consider installing a burglar alarm.

- The most secure holiday homes are those villas or apartments on a modern development which has its own security personnel as part of the package. You will pay for this in the purchase price, and the levy of a service charge.
- If you want a traditional holiday home, and security is higher on your list of priorities than privacy, consider buying a property in a village.
- When you are choosing a property, take into account the fact that you, or members of your family or friends who will use it, could find its location a little too isolated on a dark night. A superb site in the depths of the country, or on a lonely clifftop, could change character once the sun has set.
- Security also involves taking into account the political stability of a country. In times of unrest, your dream house could be subject to looting and vandalism, or hostility from local people.

Boat-houses, water-mills, lock-keepers' cottages and romantic fishing lodges make delightful holiday homes, but they will undoubtedly require renovation. The conversion of a waterside building is rarely plain sailing: good insulation and damp course are essential and may be required before money can be borrowed for the property.

Whatever their condition, waterside homes are in the upper price range of the market, for the appeal of a stretch of river, stream, or lake keeps prices buoyant. A first-class survey must be done since waterside buildings are susceptible to damp and decay.

You usually own the land to the water's edge of your property, seldom the water itself. Laws concerning fishing rights and moorings are complex and vary enormously between countries, states and even districts. For example, in France you will never own the stream on your land, and you will probably find that anyone with a fishing licence has the right to fish there, as anglers do in Ireland. In Scotland you may discover that a substantial investment, on top of the purchase price of a property, is required to secure your right to fish on a stream on your property, or you may not be able to buy that right at any price. Angling clubs sometimes have the rights to the waterfront on the property.

Waterside homes are best avoided altogether if young children are to be left to play alone. The water's edge can be fenced off and strict rules can be introduced, but parents should consider the additional stress of possible accidents when making their choice of holiday home. The tranquillity of a site is no compensation for constant worries about your children's safety. Inside the holiday home, you will be more relaxed about the standard of furnishings and decor, but do not allow a lower standard of safety precautions.

Your waterside holiday home could be a floating one. Old barges, narrowboats and houseboats are often advertised for sale in newspapers, boatyards, marinas, yachting magazines, and through yacht brokers.

Insurance for any boat or mobile home will be high. If a boat is to be occupied at any time of the year, it is in effect a houseboat. Houseboats require residential moorings with services such as electricity, sewage disposal and piped water. Check your security of tenure and remember that moorings are liable for local tax and rate charges.

If you want a sailing boat rather than a houseboat remember that it will have to be taken out of the water in the winter and then stored at great expense. Finding a mooring can be a problem unless you buy a boat which has security of tenure for its mooring as part of the deal. If it is connected to a marina development you will have good facilities and security, but at a price.

Purell Point, Canada

ANGLER'S SHACK ON FISH RIVER

This fisherman's haunt by a peaceful stretch of the river in New South Wales, Australia, was built over 130 years ago. It was originally an inn offering shelter to travellers during the gold rush at nearby Bathurst, when prospectors panned for gold in the Blue mountains. Today, it provides a perfect solitary retreat for anglers. Pictured beneath a rain-washed sky, on a day when the fishermen have left the gate open in their haste to cast the waters, it looks like an old uninhabited shack. In fact, it is still used today as a base for fishing holidays. The original corrugated iron roof, on which the rainwater drums like a tintinnabulation, before running off along the grooves, is so effective that the building is completely watertight. Inside there is no sign of damp, or watermarks staining the walls. In a cylindrical tank outside, water collects, and from here it is pumped into the house for domestic use.

The interior is very orderly compared with the ramshackle exterior. Newly whitewashed plaster walls are hung with framed charts of the river and survey maps of the area. The white painted ceiling boards are supported upon solid jarrah timber beams – the hardwood indigenous to Australia. Dominating the living room is a huge fireplace, its smoke-blackened surround providing proof of the many meals cooked here over the years. Skillets for fish are strung up on rafters nearby, and grids are placed over the embers for boiling cans of water. There is no electricity, so cooking is done over a portable gas stove in summer and, in winter, on the fire. The large, deep-set brick fireplace absorbs the heat from the fire and stays warm long after the logs have turned to ashes.

In this room there is evidence of the enthusiastic pursuit of fishing in the line-up of condiments in the bleached corner cupboard, the billycan for anglers' tucker, and the light on the fireplace surround for night fishing expeditions. On the bare plank floor stands a solid wooden table and four quirky chairs, each with a carved bracket support between the seat and the back rest for comfort. These simple pieces of furniture typify the unpretentious furnishing favoured by the owners, in sympathy with the workmanlike finish of the builders. Completely free of clutter, this is a humble dwelling where nothing is superfluous.

1 *Nearby river for trout fishing*
2 *Approach to the property*
3 *Living room with large fireplace*

3

1

2

DUTCH SAILHOUSE

A modern house at Vinkeveen outside Amsterdam was built as a weekend retreat for a family of enthusiastic sailors and windsurfers. Dutch architect, Cees Dam, planned the house carefully, drawing attention to the proximity of the water with the small round stepping stones that lead from the front door to the edge of the lake. This is bordered by a marshy garden of mallow, Queen Anne's lace and wild cornflowers. To emphasize the vertical lines of the rectangular house, there are four full-length glass doors, with decorative full-length blinds. The house, both inside and out, is a subtle monochrome of grey green, reflecting the colour of the watery landscape, with charcoal and white used as accent colours. The only covering on the grey ceramic tiled floor inside is a large mat for wiping wet or muddy boots, dripping boards or keels and wet suits. Above, on the white painted joists, sails and surfboards are stored out of the way. Within this lofty space; a side gallery houses four berths.

In the counter kitchen, there are a few nautical touches, such as the brass flap handles on the custom-built units, and the bold blue cooker ventilation hood that recalls a ship's funnel. On the charcoal worktop in the kitchen is a modern lamp with a white glass shade, shaped like a shell.

The furniture is in keeping with the clean lines of this modern house. Lacquered red chairs, with brass studded headrests, were designed by Cees Dam and these, together with the modern canvas recliner on a tubular steel frame and the white dining table, are more appropriate in these surroundings than floral patterned sofas and reproduction period pieces.

Essentially a summerhouse, the architect designed it to give maximum lake frontage, and a functional decorative scheme that would suit the owners' leisure activities.

1 *Exterior*
2 *Kitchen*
3 *Dining room showing rafters for storing sails*

1

2

3

AMERICAN LAKESIDE STUDIO

Though this lakeside studio in Ithaca, New York State, is smaller than most city apartments, the space is not restrictive. The designers, Simon Ungers and Laszlo Kiss, have built a rooftop temple above the single room to give it added stature. The A-frame construction with its timber pillars is reached by stairs, and from the top there is an unobstructed view of the water that is fringed with reeds and grasses, golden in the late summer sun. The breeze that comes off Lake Cayuga cools the open-air pavilion, which also acts as a landmark for sailors out in their boats.

The outer wall of the studio is clad with trellis to give a pergola effect, and cornerstones, painted white against the cream brick walls, sharpen the edges of the building in true modernist style. During the day there is an interesting interaction of light and shade in this treetop place and, at night, it is illuminated by beams of light that are directed upwards.

The designers have extended the walls beyond the high ceilings, which are supported on columns. This galleried effect is emphasized by the symmetrical line-up of blue panes of glass set high up on the walls above ceiling level. To make the most of the space inside the studio, much of the furniture is built-in. Platform seating neatly divides the areas for living, sleeping and cooking and a trellised screen acts as a partition between the kitchen and the living room, echoing the trellis on the outside wall of the studio. Furnishings are in warm, vibrant colours against plain white walls: a brick red carpet is covered with Persian rugs, and Indian print cushions in vegetable dye shades of ochre, sienna and sand are scattered on the seating platforms. Earthenware pots containing dried reeds and grasses from the lakeside, bring images of the surrounding countryside into focus inside the studio.

1 *Open-air pavilion on top of the house*
2 *Studio and pavilion*
3 *Living room*

1

DACHA IN FINLAND

This splendid old family house with a river frontage on a peninsula in Western Finland, has changed very little since the end of the last century. The house, surrounded by parkland, is ideal for a large family and there is plenty of room inside for guests. The present owners are descendants of the family who built the house in 1882, when Finland was a province of Tsarist Russia. All along the Baltic coast and the archipelago of the gulf of Bothnia, these villas, called 'dachas' by the Russians, were built as summer houses for St. Petersburg society. For although the Russian empire was in rapid decline, Tsar Nicholas II, who moored his yacht offshore, was unaware of the growing disquiet at home.

Built for summers by the lake, and ice-skating in winter when it froze over, this period villa is a reminder of how the upper middle classes lived in the nineteenth century.

It has kept its original character without becoming a museum. Only small modifications have been made in this technological age: the kitchen has been fully modernized and a swimming pool added in the grounds. At the time the house was built, Finland was going through a phase of romantic nationalism, which was celebrated in the art and architecture of the period. The romantic style is seen here in the intricately carved balconies, the decorative garden pavilion and the small white bridges along the river frontage. A footpath leads from the house to a bench and swing seat at the water's edge, offering a peaceful place to sit and relax at the end of the day. Viewed from the water, the golden yellow building – with its white balconies and balustrades, stands out amongst the pendulous trees.

Effective insulation is a matter to be taken seriously this far north, where winter holds the land in an icy grip for eight months of the year, so windows and doors are cased, and thick double doors protect against heavy snowfall.

Inside, a neutral colour scheme of grey and creamy white has been used in the living room, the only splashes of colour provided by the floor coverings and houseplants. There are white painted shelves, stacked with books, and pictures decorating the walls. One of these is a painting of the front of the house, seen from the river. A rocking chair, facing the window, gives the room an informal, relaxed air. This decorative scheme was introduced by the first owner of the house who painted all the wooden surfaces white (even the mahogany furniture), to give a bright, restful atmosphere to the house.

The Empire-style furniture that fills the house is also found in the wooden garden pavilion, which more obviously reflects the nineteenth century romantic style. The decorative wall panelling, which depicts romantic scenes of fashionable ladies and gentlemen, was painted by Tove Jansson, one of the most popular Finnish artists of the nineteenth century. The panels were washed in pale

1 *House from the river*

blue and columns were painted in a rich cream with a fine blue outline. The Empire style bench seat, popular in Scandinavian countries, is covered in the palest pink and white gingham, the colours matched by the finely patterned chair fabric, a rag rug in lavender and grey, and the pretty tablecloth with a bowl of bright pink geraniums set in the centre. A Japanese paper-pleated umbrella, put to unconventional use as a light shade, completes the formal interior.

In this house, where time seems to have stood still, the owners, full of vitality, continue to organize boating parties, picnics and dances, just as their ancestors did before them. But there is no false note in their effort to honour the past; every aspect of the house is appropriate and compatible. Nowadays, a television aerial is considered more relevant than a flagpole, but the family who live in this waterside house still keep the flag flying outside their traditional holiday home.

2 *Living room*
3 *Garden pavilion*

2

3

1

BOATHOUSE ON THE LOIRE

A wigwam-shaped house, afloat on a pontoon at the Erdre tributary of the Loire, is a tourist attraction. Moored in the centre of Nantes, on the west coast of France, the houseboat is provocative and challenging, admired by some, objected to by others. But entirely admirable is the technical feat of the architect, Eric Boucher. When the scheme took shape in 1980, he was still a student and thought that building his own home was preferable to looking for student digs. With help from a banker, a timber merchant, and a sanitation expert, he resolved the problem of keeping a self-contained house afloat on the river, without it being subject to building regulations. Building a new home, especially on a prime waterside site, can be fraught with difficulty, but Boucher's design circumvented the rules governing land and shipping since it is on a mooring and there is no motor or sail on board. He named the houseboat 'Odysseus', not because he will ever make a voyage in it, but because it took him out of troubled waters. Now it is the headquarters of the architectural practice he has set up with a young team who have been commissioned to plan a holiday resort in Senegal.

The plywood platform measures about 16 metres by 7 metres (51ft × 22ft), and is waterproofed with plastic resin and layered with polyester. It rests on eight cylindrical floats, strapped in pairs, which can support eight times the 15 ton weight imposed on them by the house. The reinforced floats were given a buoyancy certificate from the River Navigation Services. Four cedarwood strips form the ribbed carcass that is fitted with glass panels and clad on the outside with felt tarmac and red cedar shingle. Inside, the platform is lined with parquet flooring and the walls are insulated with glass fibre, which is covered with pine to give a mellow glow to the interior. A hatch with indoor access creates a storage tank with a 2000 litre capacity in which water can be stored, or wine at an ideal temperature of 11-12 degrees centigrade.

Light streams in through large curved windows and portholes, and the glass wall which takes up a third of the roof on one side of the house. This is used as a greenhouse for plants that are trained up the walls. An integrated micro-purifying system treats the sewage and, after one complete cycle, it turns out purified water, which is used to nourish the philodendrons and ferns.

An open-plan living area beneath the vaulted ceiling makes the interior more spacious at ground level, and

includes a kitchen that is larger than the usual ship's galley. Two mezzanine floors at the gable ends house the bedroom and bathroom, simply connected by a wooden bridge.

Heating is always an important consideration for a houseboat, and solar panels are used here to store warmth from the sun for hot water and heating in winter. The energy-saving building with its waterside mooring is an interesting venture for anyone considering a holiday home, since both the building and maintenance are inexpensive.

1 *Houseboat and mooring*
2 *Exterior at night*
3 *Kitchen and dining area*

1

BELVEDERE ON LAKE COMO

Towering above Lake Como in Italy is an unusual holiday home, the Villa Gaeta. The rooftop belvedere is level with the church steeples and campanile bell towers of Santa Abbondio di Acquaseria, and from here there is a spectacular view of the lake and surrounding countryside. The garden is formally planted with shrubs, punctuated by tall dark cypress trees.

The tower was turned into a residence without altering the external structure of nineteenth-century brick and stone, or the wood and tiled roof. But the open-air belvedere has been enclosed with glass, like a conservatory, so that it can be used as a living room, with adjoining bedroom. The entrance is marked by bright blue double doors with a wrought iron griffin hook on either side.

Originally there were only two levels inside – the ground floor and the roof, with a staircase to link them. When restoration work began, the look-out tower could only be reached by the birds, since the staircase was in a state of collapse. Two intermediate floors were built, one to house a kitchen, the other a bathroom, and the ground floor entrance has become the main storage area with large custom-built cupboards to hide any clutter. The pale parchment decoration is light in contrast to the imposing grey stone of the tower. Stippled cream walls are outlined with white painted wood, timber ceiling boards are exposed and coconut matting covers the floor. Against this natural background, furniture such as the laminated beech chairs and the bird's eye maple shelf, is sculptural.

The tower is sparsely furnished throughout and, because of limited floor space, much of the furniture is built in so that the interior does not appear too cramped. On the outside, a hoist was installed to haul up cumbersome pieces of furniture too wide for the narrow wooden staircase.

1 *Approach to the villa*
2 *Doors opening to patio*
3 *Interior*

HOUSEBOATS IN KASHMIR

'Paradise on earth' is how Kashmir was described by one of the earliest travel writers, the Moghul Emperor Jehangir, in the seventeenth century. 'A delightful flower bed, a garden of eternal springs' he enthused in his memoirs, even though it took the Mogul court three weeks to reach the enchanted vale beneath the snow-capped Himalayas – a weary trek from the hot flat plains for the palanquinned elephants.

Today, there are two flights a day to Srinagar, the capital of Kashmir, from most major cities in India. Life there still revolves around the tourists who stay in the houseboats on the fringes of four lakes – Dal, Nagin, Manasbal and Wular. The boats were introduced by the British in the days of the Empire, when *firinghis* (foreigners) were unable to buy land in India. They named their boats just as they did their suburban homes, and the Kashmiris continue the tradition with 'Noah's Ark', and 'Hollywood' to cater for all tastes.

Hand-carved in the fragrant deodar pine of the Himalayas, these fantasy palaces offer luxurious comfort to the visitor. There are bathrooms with tubs and modern plumbing, four poster beds carved in walnut, rosewood furniture, carpets and drapes with crewel-worked poppies or paisley patterns. A typical houseboat is between 80 and 125 feet long with at least six rooms to accommodate two or three families. The top deck is a terrace for viewing the lake. Everyone takes to the water in Kashmir: even farmers tend their crops of fruit, vegetables and flowers on floating rafts of soil, layered between willow branches. These fertile gardens are known as *rads*. At dawn each morning, just as the sun washes the misty lakes with the first pink light, the market boats assemble with the produce, while the flower seller paddles silently past on his skiff that is filled with the white lilies, tuber roses and golden ranunculus for which Kashmir is famous.

Punts and houseboat in Kashmir

1

2

3

ENGLISH CANAL BOATS

For over two centuries narrow cargo boats plied the English canals, but when railway tracks replaced the canal network, many were converted to holiday homes. Nowadays, horse-powered engines, rather than horses, keep the boats on the move.

The decorative tradition of the narrowboat is still observed today: boldly painted scenes of fairytale castles and garlands of flowers cover the inside and outside of the barges. These motifs are painted with such individuality that a boatman can recognize which yard a boat has come from. The colourful tin utensils, replicas of implements from the East, were brought on board by the boatmen. China plates, threaded with ribbon, are fastened to the walls of the barges. These customary adornments go back to the days when the narrowboats were used to bring clay to the Staffordshire kilns, and china was made for them in return.

1-4 *English narrowboats* 4

INDEX

ACKNOWLEDGMENTS

*The publisher thanks the following photographers and organizations
for their kind permission to reproduce the pictures in this book:*

2-3 Derry Moore, courtesy of Architectural Digest; **6-7** Finnish Tourist Board/Hannu Vallas Rypsipelto; **10** Michael Boys; **12-15** The World of Interiors/Fritz von der Schulenburg; **16-19** Elizabeth Whiting & Associates/Tim Street-Porter; **20-21** Tim Stephens; **22-25** La Maison de Marie Claire/Sarramon/de Roquette; **26-27** Conran Octopus/Simon Brown; **28-31** John Vaughan; **32-35** Michael Boys; **36-37** Bent Rej; **38-39** Lars Hallen; **40-41** Derry Moore, courtesy of Architectural Digest; **44** Bent Rej; **46-47** Derry Moore, courtesy of Architectural Digest; **48-51** Top Agence/Roland Beaufre; **52-53** Bent Rej; **54-55** La Maison de Marie Claire/Chabaneix/Rozensztroch; **56-57** Conran Octopus/Simon Brown; **58-59** Bent Rej; **60-61** Vogue Living/John Hay; **62-65** Elizabeth Whiting & Associates/Tim Street-Porter; **66-69** Ron Sutherland; **70-71** Derry Moore; **72-73** Vogue Living/John Hay; **74-75** Conran Octopus/Simon Brown; **76-77** Vogue Living/Anthony Browell; **78-79** La Maison de Marie Claire/Mouries/Sabarros; **80-83** Vogue Living/John Hay; **84-85** Robert Harding Picture Library/Andrew Besley; **88** Bent Rej; **90-91** Karen Bussolini/Miki Boro; **92-93** Bent Rej; **94-95** Camera Press; **96-97** Raghubir Singh; **98-99** Top Agence/Pascal Hinous; **100-103** John Hay; **104-105** Zefa Picture Library; **109** Daily Telegraph Colour Library/Barrett and MacKay; **110-111** Vogue Living/John Hay; **112-113** John Vaughan; **114-115** Karen Bussolini; **116-119** Lars Hallen; **120-121** La Maison de Marie Claire/Pratt/Doussy; **122-123** Abitare/Antonia Mulas; **124-125** Tejbir Singh; **126-127** Michael Boys.